PSYCHOANALYTIC INQUIRY
A Topical Journal for Mental Health Professionals

Volume 6   1986   Number 1

CONTENTS

On Power

Routledge
Taylor & Francis Group
New York London

Routledge is an imprint of the
Taylor & Francis Group, an informa business

PSYCHOANALYTIC INQUIRY

Editor-in-Chief
JOSEPH D. LICHTENBERG, M.D.

Editors
MELVIN BORNSTEIN, M.D.   DONALD SILVER, M.D.

ISSN 0735-1690

Psychoanalytic Inquiry is issued quarterly by The Analytic Press. Distributed solely by Lawrence Erlbaum Associates, Inc., 365 Broadway, Hillsdale, New Jersey 07642. Annual subscription rate for individuals is $39.50; for institutions, $60.00. Annual rate for subscribers located outside of the U.S.A. and Canada for individuals is $48.50; for institutions, $69.00. Individual issues are available prepaid at $15.00 each (postage included).

Prologue

ALTHOUGH THE PROBLEM OF POWER in mental life and human interaction has an important place in many psychosocial models, it has remained the stepchild of psychoanalysis. The phenomenology and explanatory value of power is too important to remain tangential and ambiguous within psychoanalysis. To find a significant place for the concept of power in psychoanalytic theory has been difficult since power implies a holistic and interactional viewpoint. These viewpoints cannot be easily reconciled with either a drive conflict or a deficit model.

We envision this issue of *Psychoanalytic Inquiry* as a pioneering effort, a beginning examination of the dimensions of power in psychoanalytic thought. We invited five contributors to address the problem of power. The result is a heterogeneous group of papers varying from studies of powerful historical figures to a reformulation of metapsychology.

In "Male Sexuality and Power," Ethel Person proposes a new perspective on male power and sexuality. She takes issue with the view that aggression, phallic sadism, and castration anxiety are fundamental to male sexual fantasies and conflicts. She argues that a decisive role in male power also centers on narcissistic issues such as the fear of powerlessness in the control of the penis and the fear of loss of the love object.

Peter Loewenberg, in "Nixon, Hitler, and Power," applies an ego psychology approach to the careers of two powerful politicians to suggest the variety and richness of psychoanalytic formulations that are now available to the psychohistorian.

"The Relationship of Psychosexual Development to the Successful Excercise of Power in a Woman Ruler: A Study of Catherine dé Medici," by Abby Adams-Silvan and Mark Silvan, uses a biographical study of Catherine dé Medici to demonstrate how women who

1

rule do not have to rely on the use of male identifications to be effective. Rather, the effectiveness of female leaders can more reliably be achieved through the attainment of mature *feminine psychosexual development.*

Helen Gediman, in "The Plight of the Imposturous Candidate: Learning Amidst the Pressures and Pulls of Power in the Institute," addresses the situation of the candidate within a psychoanalytic institute. The candidate must deal with the power of the institute's organizational and educational hierarchy and to do so must develop an adaptive identification with an individual in power roles. This adaptive effort will go awry for a candidate who has imposturous tendencies. Gediman fortifies her argument with the description of a candidate for whom the complexity of the power relationships provoked a regression to an imposturous stance.

James Grotstein argues that the problem of power is the fundamental problem of psychopathology. In "The Psychology of Powerlessness," he develops a model of psychopathology that is based upon deficits expressed phenomenologically as states of powerlessness in maintaining proper regulatory activity. Instinctual drives, rather than being the source of mental activity and psychopathology, function as regulators. Accordingly, the basic state of disregulation is experienced as randomness, meaninglessness and dissolution.

Finally, in addition to discussing the preceding papers, Bennett Simon draws attention to the need to consider the meaning of power in the analyst's personal, professional, and political life. He describes how the authors of the papers demonstrate the varied dimensions of a psychoanalytic consideration of power from the limited explanatory power of a psychoanalytic interpretation of a historical figure to the great generalizing power of a psychoanalytic interpretation in human development. Furthermore, Simon suggests that the papers considered together demonstrate power is not a unitary concept but is so variable that it is impossible to claim that there are psychoanalytic perspectives of power.

Melvin Bornstein, M.D.
Issue Editor

Male Sexuality and Power

ETHEL S. PERSON, M.D.

MALE PSYCHOLOGY IS BEGINNING TO ATTRACT the kind of attention paid to its female counterpart over the past 15 years. However, while the assumption that female sexual masochism is primary, universal, and defining has been challenged, the popular belief that male sexuality is innately aggressive and sadistic has persisted with minimal questioning.

The cultural stereotype of male sexuality is of a kind of phallic omnipotence and supremacy, a phallus invested with the power of mastery. At the very least, this macho view depicts a large, powerful, untiring phallus attached to a very cool male, long on self-control, experienced, competent, and knowledgeable enough to make women crazy with desire. As Zilbergeld has said "It's two feet long, hard as steel, and can go all night" (1978, p. 23). In the shared cultural fantasy, even the normally reticent female is perceived to be utterly powerless and receptive when confronted by pure macho sexuality.

But phallic power is also viewed as easily corrupted into sexual domination and violence. This is clear in the common depiction of male sexuality in pornography, movies, TV, and sexual humor, and in much of the major fiction of our time.

Ethel S. Person, M.D., is Director and Training and Supervising Analyst, Columbia University Center for Psychoanalytic Training and Research; Professor of Clinical Psychiatry, Department of Psychiatry, Columbia University, College of Physicians and Surgeons. Earlier versions of this paper were presented at the William Alanson White Institute, September 19, 1984 and as "The Foundation Lecture" for the New Jersey Psychoanalytic Society, November 15, 1984. I thank Drs. Robert Michels and Arnold Rothstein, who read an earlier version of this paper and made extremely cogent suggestions.

Although Kate Millet's *Sexual Politics* (1970) is certainly one of the seminal books in the feminist movement, it is essentially a study of male psychology and a condemnation of the power motive perceived in male sexuality. She analyzes the work of four distinguished male authors whose descriptions of male sexuality centered on ideas of ascendancy and power: Henry Miller, D. H. Lawrence, Norman Mailer, and Jean Genet. According to Millett, "As one recalls both the euphemism and the idealism of descriptions of coitus in the Romantic Poets (Keats's *Eve of Saint Agnes*) or the Victorian novelists (Hardy, for example) and contrasts it with Miller or William Burroughs, one has an idea of how contemporary literature has absorbed not only the truthful explicitness of pornography, but its anti-social character as well. Since this tendency to hurt or insult has been given free expression, it has become far easier to assess sexual antagonism in the male" (1970, p. 46). Zilbergeld quotes Harold Robbins, Mickey Spillane, Henry Miller, Norman Mailer, James Baldwin, and still others to make the same points about the ways in which our culture sees male sexuality as domineering and even violent.

There is currently a genre of popular fiction in which the common thread is heroic, macho, adventurous, and virile. The male preoccupation with this type of literature is comparable to that of women with the romance novel. The female novels are so popular that the word "harlequin," taken from the publishing house of the same name, has become a descriptive noun. I would suggest that the equivalent term for the male novel might be "herotica."

A passage from Eric van Lustbader's *The Miko* captures the way male sexuality is portrayed in this growing body of writing. The plot hinges on the idea that Akiko, a woman trained in the arcane mystic and martial arts, is sworn to avenge a loved one and kill the hero, Nicholas. She is portrayed as a master assassin in perfect control of all her feelings, but her response to Nicholas compels her to have a sexual encounter with him:

> For the first time in her life Akiko was open to the universe. Nothing in all her long arduous training had caused this ignition inside of her.

She was so dizzy that she was doubly grateful for his strong arms about her. All breath had left her as he had uttered her name, how she ached for him! Her thighs were like water, unable to support her. She felt a kind of ecstasy at his touch she thought only possible in orgasm. What was happening to her? Swept away, still a dark part of her mind yammered to be heard. What strange force had invaded her mind? What turned her plans of vengeance inside out? What made her feel this way about a hated enemy? [p. 277].

In one remarkable example of "herotica," the hero is so well schooled in the erotic arts that if he hates a woman and wishes to destroy her forever, he makes love to her so skillfully that she knows that she will never be satisfied by any other man.[1]

Observers from diverse disciplines have suggested either that macho sexuality is sanctioned as the cultural ideal or, conversely, that it accurately portrays male sexuality. May (1980, p. 131) suggested that in addition to the cultural directive for males to be assertive in general, "the popular prescription for male sexuality is also heavily invested with assertion and activity. The man is supposed to be constantly on the move and on the make. The image of the tireless seducer differs only in style and degree from that of the rapist." The only question is whether the male attracts and seduces the female or overpowers and forces her. May's view echoes that of Susan Brownmiller (1976). In her book *Against Our Will: Men, Women and Rape,* she declares: "Throughout history no theme grips the masculine imagination with greater constancy and less honor than the myth of the heroic rapist. As man conquered the world, so too he conquers the female. Down through the ages, imperial conquest, exploits of valor and expressions of love have gone hand in hand with violence to women in thought and in deed" (p. 320).

As already noted, there is an assumption, particularly in some of the feminist literature, that the pervasive macho image accurately reflects an individual male's preoccupation with sexual domination

---

[1]Unfortunately, I abandoned this book on a boat and so cannot supply the actual reference.

and violence. Sexual violence, including wife abuse, marital rape, and rape, is regarded as the tip of the iceberg, an indicator of the innate male propensity to sexual sadism. This position postulates a continuum between male sexual violence and normal male sexuality.

Yet there has been no systematic attempt to assess the pervasiveness of the macho stereotype as an ego ideal in individual men, or any effort to gauge the extent of domination as a male fantasy preoccupation. One question that naturally arises is the relationship of the cultural stereotype of macho sexuality to the interior fantasy life of men. Moreover, the larger question is whether the domination and sadism fantasies and impulses that one does see are primary. Is male sexuality inherently aggressive, or are the aggressive fantasies a reaction to life experiences or compensation for feelings of inadequacy?

In this paper I challenge the popular cultural notion that male sexuality is by its nature aggressive. To some degree, conscious male sexual fantasies, as revealed in both clinical work and nonclinical survey studies, do resemble the cultural stereotype. But there are significant differences. First of all, sexual violence and aggression are not primary fantasy themes for many males. Some men do not have fantasies of sexual domination. Control both of the sexual apparatus and of the partner takes precedence in the fantasies of a significant portion of the population.

Furthermore, it would be naive to restrict one's conclusions about male sexuality to conscious wishful fantasies alone. Fearful fantasies must also be taken into account in assessing the overall nature of male sexuality. Taken together, they present a more balanced picture. Wishful fantasies are often about domination and aggression, but they are also about size, hardness, endurance, skill, and willing females. Fears are partly the negative reflections of the wishful fantasies; as such, they focus on inadequate penis size, impotence, lack of skill, fear of female rejection, female damage to the male (vagina dentata fantasies), and homosexual dread. (While unconscious fears do not appear to be fantasies, at least not to those who experience them, they are clearly fantasies or fantasy derivatives.) Most important, data from analyses reveal the unconscious fantasies of patients that underlie conscious wishful and fearful fantasies and suggest the correspondence of unconscious fantasies to developmental events.

The pervasiveness of the dominant and aggressive theme of male sexual fantasies — and the macho image in general — may represent a shared cultural ideal to some degree, but it is only ego-syntonic or an actual personal ego ideal for a minority of men. Those men for whom sexual domination is a primary concern generally reveal particular conflicts in their sexual development. However, the nature and origin of their unconscious conflicts as revealed in psychoanalyses point to the universal "fault" lines in more typical (or "normal") male development.

Drawing on conscious male wishful and fearful fantasies and some clinical material that reveals the interplay of macho sexuality and sexual fears, I am here attempting to place power and domination concerns in perspective by proposing that control over the penis and the sexual object are central concerns in male sexuality, more fundamental than aggression, and intimately intertwined with the genesis of castration anxiety. The emphasis on the power of the phallus and power remedies vis-á-vis the female (or male) partner are, at least in part, compensatory responses to anxieties engendered in the male developmental experience. These anxieties must be understood as an amalgam of castration anxiety, fear and envy of both sexes, and the fear (or experience) of loss of the object and loss of love.

My focus is on some of the sources of the central anxieties concerning control that have been less extensively explored than castration anxiety. The case material I present suggests one set of developmental factors that predisposes men, on the one hand, to unusually intense sexual anxiety and fear of loss of the object and, on the other hand, to sexual dominance and macho sexuality as compensatory mechanisms. Male sexual aggression may be almost universal, but it is a transitory and generally inconsequential stage in childhood unless it is reinvoked and consolidated in a series of power strategies as a defense against an amalgam of sexual anxieties. In this respect, male sexual aggression may be viewed as analogous to primary and secondary female sexual masochism.

Conscious Fantasies

Fantasy life is extremely varied, and sexual fantasies are no exception. Among men, the wide range (even within our one culture) is well documented in popular books and professional journals. But despite this variability, there are fundamental differences between male and female fantasy life.[2]

Unlike female sexual fantasies, which may be diffusively romantic, male fantasies are usually explicitly sexual and often impersonal; autonomy, mastery, and physical prowess are central concerns (May, 1980). They frequently portray domination, as the widespread rape, control, and transgression themes would indicate. But although domination is unquestionably a major motif, male fantasies may also be passive, submissive, or masochistic in content. In fact, Freud first described "feminine" masochism as it occurred in men (1924).

There are other male fantasies that are at least as common, possibly more so. Two of the most common are fantasies of "the omni-available woman" and "Lesbian" sex. The omni-available woman is totally accessible. She is often fantasized as lying on a couch awaiting the arrival of her lover, forever lubricated, forever ready, forever desiring. Both from my own patients' reports and from reading through the popular and scientific reports of fantasies, it seems evident that, for men the woman's availability, ready sexuality, and unqualified approval constitute a major common thread. It is her availability and enthusiasm that bolster his virility.

---

[2]The only major statistical analysis of fantasies remains that of Kinsey et al. (1948, 1953). They discovered that not only the content but also the formal attributes of sexual fantasies vary with gender. For example, most males fantasize during masturbation and have nocturnal sex dreams. In contrast, fantasy among females is much more variable. Females tend to fantasize about what has actually occurred; males more frequently fantasize about unfulfilled desires. (Kinsey's group also noted some social class differences that alert us to the fact that fantasies from any one sample are not easily generalized.)

Barclay (1973), in a study on the sexual fantasies of college men and women noted that "male fantasies sounded like features of *Playboy* magazine or pornographic books, and included elaborate descriptions of the imagined sexual partner. . . they were stereotyped . . . without personal involvement. Women are always seductive and straightforward, ready to have intercourse at any given time . . . [with a] major emphasis on visual imagery" (p. 205).

In men's fantasies, women are viewed as desirable, but dispensable. In contrast, as Thorne (1971) points out, women see themselves as both desirable and indispensable.

Young boys, prepubescent and pubescent, commonly have fantasies about naked girls available to them in such powerless positions as being bound to a bed (Thorne, 1971). These may or may not contain elements of sadism, but often do (Lukianowicz, 1960). A young boy's sexual fantasies are mainly involved with exploration and discovery of female anatomy. They are colored by a literal preoccupation with girls. Boys seem generally to fantasize about the sexual compliance of girls or about sexual advances from them. In these fantasies, girls don't complain about the bad treatment they may be getting, but gratefully accept the status of sexual toys.

The same themes continue to be found in young men, although some of the overt force may be reduced. It is the developmental significance of the change in male fantasies as boys grow older—the partial replacement of physical dominance as a theme by that of the presence of a bevy of willing females—that suggests these fantasies are on a continuum. The common feature is the insurance of the sexual availability of the female. The wish is that girls are really panting for sex; in extreme cases, this accounts for the common defense in rape trials—"she was really asking for it."

Forcing a partner is one way of insuring her presence. The fantasy of domination, in its intent, seems to be on a continuum with the fantasied presence of a woman in a perpetual state of sexual readiness, with no other aim than to await the man's sexual advances. Nancy Friday, in her study of write-in fantasies (1980), found that the largest single fantasy category for men was that of sadomasochistic sex. But she noted that the intent was not usually to hurt the woman, only that she enjoy the encounter. This fantasy, in its intent, seems to be on a continuum with the fantasied presence of a woman in a perpetual state of sexual readiness, with no other purpose than to receive the man's sexual advances. Control of the woman, even in domination fantasies, is most often in the service of phallic narcissism. It may also protect against the potential threat of castration from the woman. Only rarely is the point to harm the woman for the sake of sadism and violence per se.

The Fantasy Project at the Columbia Psychoanalytic Center for Training and Research (Person et al., 1985), designed to study sexual fantasies and behaviors utilizing a questionnaire format, has analyzed data from 193 students. The somewhat striking results suggest greater predilection for dominance among males, as compared to women, but this group of fantasies is among the less frequently reported for *both* sexes. Eleven percent of the men reported fantasies of torturing a sexual partner and 20 percent of whipping or beating a sexual partner, but 44 percent fantasied forcing a partner to submit to sexual acts. The comparable figures for women are 0 percent, 1 percent, and 10 percent.

Yet what is just as striking as the sex difference is the number of men who do not report any conscious fantasies of domination (56 percent). Furthermore, far fewer men report fantasies of actual violence or torture than report domination. We have not tested the results of an older population, but I would guess there would be progressively fewer fantasies of overt force with increasing age.

Another prominent feature of the erotic fantasy life of heterosexual men is its preoccupation with Lesbian themes. Although heterosexuals of both sexes fantasize homosexual sex with members of their own sex, essentially only heterosexual men also fantasize homosexual sex involving the opposite sex. Fantasies that focus on Lesbian sex have two major variants. In the first, the sexual encounter is exclusively between the women; in the second, the women are joined either by a male onlooker or a male participant. These fantasies appear to be on a continuum; the transitional fantasy between Lesbian sex and threesome sex is the fantasy in which the male is initially onlooker, then joins in the sex-play. A scene depicting Lesbian sex is so much a part of pornographic movies intended for heterosexual men that it is almost a convention of such films. The visual depiction of Lesbian sex seems to arouse even men who do not have the fantasy independently. In part, the fantasy of two women making love suggests an overabundance of women whose primary interest and sole function is sexual, insuring that the man will never be humiliated by the absence of a sexual object.[3] At this level, the fantasy is one variant of the fantasy of the omni-available woman. Like fantasies of women happily making love with animals having gigantic penises, or women masturbating with dildoes, Lesbian sex portrays lusty women. They cannot accuse men of being animals or dirty; they are female versions of the man's own sexual self-image.

Conscious Fears: Their Interplay with Cultural "Macho" Sexuality

As already noted, sexual fears are almost mirror images of wishes. A very large number of men feel that their penises are inadequate either in length or girth. This concern appears more widespread than female self-doubts about breast size, perhaps more closely approximating female concerns about fat. Both heterosexuals and homosexuals agonize not just about physical endowment but about performance as well. There is one significant difference: heterosexuals feel much more threatened by the appearance of another man's erect penis.

As to performance, men worry about getting it up, keeping it up, and satisfying their partners. That they frequently ask the partner "Did you come?" is testimony to this. It also betrays a basic imbalance in sex — men are stuck with the fact that their sexual excitement is visible. There is no hiding the failure to achieve an erec-

---

[3]The meaning of the male preoccupation (in fantasy and in practice) of Lesbian sex is more complex but is beyond the scope of the primary concern of this paper. In part, I think it reflects an unconscious feminine identification which is personified in the image of one or the other of the women.

tion and no certain way to gauge the woman's sexual arousal or orgasm. It is difficult for a man to really know whether he is a good lover, and men are often unable to accept such a compliment or reassurance. The fear surfaces in some men's obsessions about their partners' past lovers: "Was he better?" "Did she have more orgasms? Better orgasms?" and so forth. Of those men confident in their performance, some are so intent on controlling the female that their own participation lacks spontaneity. Some men only feel comfortable pursuing their own pleasure after they have brought the woman to orgasm; some only attain full erection when the woman is sated.

The most striking feature of the male's sense of inadequacy is his belief that other men are truly in possession of macho sexuality. He feels macho sexuality is unobtainable for him personally, but not that it is a myth. In light of this belief, his own endowment and skills appear even more meager. Many men suffer because of their idealization of the male adolescent experience, the only time perpetual readiness appears to be the rule. But the overestimation of other males' sexuality appears to have its deepest roots in the oedipal boy's awe of his father's superior sexual endowment.

In order to compensate for the sense of genital inferiority, performance anxiety, and the fears of female rejection or infidelity, men resort to power remedies in fantasy. Through denial and reversal, the penis emerges as all powerful, performance as extraordinary, and sexual partners as plentiful. Dominance and aggression are reparative themes that betray another state of affairs — a fear of sexual powerlessness, female unavailability, and rejection. When I say that the male resorts to power remedies, I use the term power not in the sense of a set of impulses to defeat competitors, but in the sense of imbuing the penis with power and insuring the source of gratification by supplying a fantasized plethora of lusty women over whom the man is lord.

On one level, "macho" sexual fantasies are adaptive and counteract underlying fears; but at the same time they aggravate an already pervasive sexual anxiety, since the man literally believes other men are doing better. Thus uncertainty about his sexual process appears much more basic to male sexuality than its reputed aggressive content. This is not to deny the aggressive element, but to suggest that it is neither universal nor primary.

Living the Life: Clinical Examples of Macho Sexuality

The following four clinical vignettes are of patients who lived and idealized some version of macho sexuality entailing multiple partners, Lesbian sex, and phallic narcissism. These patients all shared certain conflicts that lie hidden behind the macho defense. While these conflicts are not synonymous with Everyman's erotic sensibility, they are suggestive of "fault" lines in male development. All these patients were periodically beset with overt outbursts of fears about sexual adequacy. The first two vignettes are extremely brief, simply examples of the different forms macho fantasies may take. The second two are rendered somewhat more fully. All of these patients were "lovers" of women, though their need to dominate and their hostility toward women were not far from the surface. None of these patients showed extreme hostility or violence to women. However, I have never had in analysis any man who fell at the violent end of the sexual spectrum. I don't think this is accidental. Such individuals are not likely to voluntarily present themselves for analytic treatment, particularly to a female therapist.

R. M.

R. M. fantasied about sex with two women simultaneously and about Lesbian sex, but he did not enact this. What he did instead was to set up his wife, his primary mistress, and an ancillary mistress in apartments within walking distance of each other. He essentially established a harem, though the women were unaware of each other. He was particularly proud of the fact that he could see his own apartment from those of his mistresses. Desite his sexual bravado, he was not infrequently impotent, an occurrence he generally attributed either to a wish to be elsewhere or to guilt. When either the wife or the primary mistress threatened to leave him, he fell completely to pieces, even going so far as to threaten suicide.

B. D.

B. D. always maintained at least two sexual relationships, both of which he considered significant. He never asked the women to have a simultaneous sexual encounter, but he did apprise each of his sexual activities with the other. He was apparently one of the extremely proficient lovers utterly devoted to the sexual fulfillment of his partners during any sexual encounter. His sexual withholding was enacted by his ostentatious alternation of weekends between the women, and his refusal to see them during the week.

M. D.

M. D. is a middle-aged writer of considerable reputation and affluence. He sought treatment at the insistence of his wife of 15 years to determine if he had problems. She felt it was a sign of his emotional liability or disability that he insisted on an open marriage, which she refused. Their relationship had gradually deteriorated, and time together was frittered away in petty power struggles with mutual withholding of sex.

In adolescence and early manhood, M. D. had a retarded sexual life, having come out of a repressive religious background, and he was monogamous in his first marriage. It was only when his first wife left him that he embarked on a totally different kind of sexual career, at this point having moved out of a sheltered conservative suburb into a more artistic and bohemian milieu. He never again pursued a monogamous path, and always had at least two female friends nearby. It was with some trepidation that he married for the second time, now with the conviction that he wouldn't be faithful. He saw his passion for multiple sexual relationships not as neurotic but as an interest in variety, a sincere appreciation of many different women. He had begun to lie to his wife to avoid conflict, but very much resented the fact that he was lying and ultimately felt that it was a bourgeois compromise.

During the treatment he became emotionally involved with another woman. However, despite his many dissatisfactions with his marriage and his new friend's willingness to share him with other women, he maintained that he could not "make it" with either. When his wife was out of town he became frightened at being alone with his mistress and arranged to see other women then as well. One of his worst fears was that he might suddenly lose all the women with whom he was involved. Being with no one seemed to him the worst fate of all.

He periodically experienced severe pain in his penis and lived in fear of the time when his sexual powers might fail. He had a dim awareness that his inability to leave his wife or attempt to ameliorate the situation betrayed a conflictual attachment.

S. M.

S. M., a professionally successful man, came into treatment because of recurrent depressions. He was extremely proud of his beautiful, well-preserved wife, and was obviously pleased at her voracious sexual appetite. Although he was morbidly jealous about lovers she had had prior to their marriage, he had initiated threesome sex primarily with one other woman, but occasionally with another man as well. He enjoyed talking about how much his wife liked these sexual encounters. He was proud of her rapture, but also because she was so clearly at his disposal. Despite her willingness to oblige, he kept a number of ancillary friends, though he in no way regarded this as unfaithfulness.

During his depressions, usually triggered by business reversals, he became impotent. This was invariably followed by an obsessive preoccupation with his wife's former relationships, pathological jealousy, and the suspicion that she was currently unfaithful. He would then reject her and accuse her of being a dog in heat.

He had a series of paired dreams with slight variations. In one of the pair, his wife was all powerful and drove a chariot while he clung to her feet and she fertilized the land with great streams of water. In the paired dream, he controlled two giant stallions and dragged his wife along behind him. These oscillations in his perception became very rapid and revealed the way in which he perceived his wife and himself as locked in a bitter struggle for power and yet yoked together.

To varying degrees, the men I have described perceived themselves as living the macho life. They played out different facets of two prominent macho fantasies: the omni-sexual woman and the fascination with Lesbian sex.

All four men had certain characteristics in common. None viewed himself as having ongoing sexual fears or concerns. In fact their sexual behavior was not only ego-syntonic but idealized as well, viewed as the emblem of true manhood. Periodically, however, each was subject to intermittent fears about the health and intactness of his penis, impotence, and the loss of a sexual partner. All described themselves and were described by their partners as being unusually proficient lovers. This proficiency, particularly in the case of B. D., was seen as an important instrument in maintaining control over their women, despite the women's objection to some of the arrangements. All had experienced what they bitterly regarded as rejections by women in adolescence or young adulthood. These experiences had not dampened their enthusiasm for women, but had made them wary of investing all their emotions in only one.

All hid their dependency needs and narcissistic vulnerability behind a fairly primitive phallic chauvinism; they symbolically controlled their women through phallic mastery and supremacy. The underlying dependence was only revealed in symptomatic outbreaks (anxiety, depression, impotence) when the relationships were on the verge of rupture.

All relied on their wives' (or girlfriends') accounts when reporting their problems to the analyst. There was an explicit belief that the wife was a better observer and reporter. However, the faithful repetition of the women's complaints, delivered in the most rational way imaginable, only gave lip service to their powers of perception; the emotional significance of the female partner's accusations was denied, given the lie behind the cool rational, sincere façade of fair-mindedness.

None of these men had intimate friendships with other men; the emotional reference points of their lives were women. In fact, they had not only excluded "fathers" from their emotional lives, but "brothers" as well. In treatment there was an attempt to establish the same covertly needy, manifestly dismissive or controlling relationship they maintained with their wives. These patients had relatively strong needs to negotiate and switch times, to stop and restart analysis, and to retaliate for the analyst's vacations. Simultaneously, they regarded the (female) analyst as powerful and phallic, though not sexual. All four analyses were distinguished by the marked absence of any well-developed erotic transference (Person, 1985).

Developmental Sources for Feelings of Sexual Inadequacy, and Fears of Female Unavailability

What is the source of the male's sense of sexual deficiency and potential "starvation"? Theories of male sexuality are somewhat skewed, focusing, as they do almost exclusively of the resolution of the positive oedipal complex. In this standard formulation, the boy avoids the threat of castration from the father by renouncing his mother; he chooses the narcissistic cathexis of his penis over the libidinal cathexis of his mother, thereby preserving and strengthening his phallic narcissism. The fundamental sexual problem for boys is viewed as the struggle to achieve phallic strength and power vis-á-vis other men. And indeed, oedipal themes and fears are explicit in male fantasy life; they are copiously revealed in conscious fantasies, dreams, and analytic associations, and leave little doubt as to their centrality to the male experience.

This formulation is accurate so far as it goes, but by focusing predominately on the father–son struggle, the threat of castration at the hands of the father, and the resolution through a powerful paternal identification, the importance of other developmental components of male sexuality is minimized.

Castration anxiety is itself obviously affected by factors other than fear of the father. It is difficult to accept a direct and exclusive link between castration anxiety (at the hands of the father) and fears of female rejection and genital inferiority. There are clearly other sources which accentuate and contribute to these anxious preoccupations.

What is missing in traditional formulations is the impact of the mother–son relationship on sexuality at different developmental stages, and the nature of the male's sexual realities at different points in the life cycle. Too often, the female is portrayed more as a prize than a protagonist in the boy's sexual development. There are important contributions to the psychoanalytic literature that focus on the effects of the mother–son relationship (Horney's 1932 paper, for example), but these studies — and the effects on male sexuality that they detail — tend to be relegated to the footnotes (the exception being studies on perversion, in which some focus on preoedipal issues is inescapable). Even so, the ample evidence of everyday life emphasizes their importance. Another variable relates to the ambiguous masculine identification seen in some men, and the degree of feminine identification that may be present. In my discussion I focus primarily on the first two factors.

Freud (1920), Horney (1932) and, more recently, some of the French theorists (McDougall, 1980; Chassequet-Smirgel, 1984) have suggested that the first blow to the boy's sexual narcissism is his *inability* to secure his mother's sexual love. In other words, the boy's fear of his father and the threat of castration (at the hands of his father) are not the only factors in the boy's renunciation of his mother. As Freud (1920) suggests, the boy also withdraws his libidinal investment from his mother because he feels he does not have the genital endowment to compete with his father. His sense is that his mother rejects him in favor of his father because his penis is too small. Brenner (1979) has made a similar point. He stresses both the narcissistic injury and the depressive affect that may be generated in the phallic-oedipal period and their connection to castration anxiety. Many men never recover from this literal sense of genital inadequacy. It appears that many men are therefore destined to suffer lifelong penis envy.

It was Horney (1932) who most fully elaborated this formulation of male sexuality:

> The anatomical differences between the sexes lead to a totally different situation in girls and in boys, and really to understand

both their anxiety and the diversity of their anxiety we must take into account first of all *the children's real situation* in the period of their early sexuality. The girl's nature as biologically conditioned gives her the desire to receive, to take into herself; she feels or knows that her genital is too small for her father's penis and this makes her react to her own genital wishes with direct anxiety: she dreads that if her wishes were fulfilled, she herself or her genital would be destroyed.

The boy, on the other hand, feels or instinctively judges that his penis is much too small for his mother's genital and reacts with the dread of his own inadequacy, of being rejected and derided. Thus he experiences anxiety which is located in quite a different quarter from the girl's; his original dread of women is not castration-anxiety at all, but a reaction to the menace of his self-respect [pp. 355–356].

As Horney notes, the boy suffers a blow to his sense of genital adequacy and consequently to his masculine self-regard. At the same time, he is reminded of earlier frustrations (oral, anal) at the hands of that same mother. Consequently, in accordance with the talion principle, "The result is that his phallic impulses to penetrate merge with his anger at frustration, and the impulses take on a sadistic tinge" (p. 356). This might be regarded as nearly universal, but essentially transient. If the anger and sadism are great, the female genital (again by virtue of the talion principle) will itself become the source of castration anxiety, and the mother, along with the father, will be seen as a potential castrator.

However, Horney observed that sexual sadism and fear of the female as castrator were not invariable among her male patients, whereas the anxiety connected to masculine self-regard was almost universal. As she puts it, "According to my experience the dread of being rejected and derided is a typical ingredient in the analysis of every man, no matter what his mentality or the structure of his neurosis" (p. 357).

Horney (p. 358) quotes Freud to the effect that the boy "behaves as if he had a dim idea that this member might be and should be larger" (Freud, 1923). She points to the continuity between the narcissistic blow to the oedipal boy and the adult man's ongoing anxiety about the size and potency of his penis. This mental set has several different components: fear that his genitals are inadequate, the corollary fear of female rejection, and a sense of the superior endowment of his rivals.

In addition to the castration anxiety engendered by the paternal rivalry, men suffer from a sense of inadequacy vis-á-vis the mother and from fear of her as well. The male's fear of the female, of his inability to please her (and his anger at her) stem from different developmental levels: fear of the preoedipal mother who abandons/engulfs, of the anal mother who intrudes/indulges, of the phallic-narcissistic-level mother who falsely seduces/denigrates masculinity, of the oedipal mother who cannot be fulfilled, rejects, falsely seduces. Out of the amalgam of potential fears arises the male propensity to compensate through sexual fantasies of power and control and through denial of his dependence on female sexual acceptance and participation.

I believe that this formulation delineates one important developmental strand in male sexuality. Yet it remains difficult to substantiate the continuity between these hypothetical childhood events and adult fears.[4] We do know though that the conjectured events are recapitulated in adolescence by virtue of the male and female adolescent's *real situation,* and again by the adult's *real situation.*

The boy's narcissistic wound — his inability to secure the object of his childhood sexual desire — is recapitulated in adolescence by the hypersexuality of the adolescent male compared to his female counterpart. The typical male adolescent experience is one of perpetual arousal with masturbation as his primary outlet. His arousal and desire come at a time when he is not equipped to easily maintain a secure sexual relationship. This discrepancy reinforces his fears about securing a sexual object and his own genital adequacy. Yet he resents the unavailability of a female partner. Since he assumes

---

[4]Although men in analysis offer many associations that demonstrate the male's sense of inadequacy vis-á-vis women and their sense of inadequate endowment, it is difficult to definitively establish the genetic source of the anxiety.

other males are doing better (a derivative of his oedipal defeat), his feelings of inferiority vis-á-vis other men are intensified.

Furthermore, the ambivalence about his control over his genital equipment and sexuality can be traced to physical aspects of the adolescent induction into genitality. In adolescence, the male is overcome with a sexual arousal over which he feels he has little control. While spontaneous erection and ejaculation are best understood as release phenomena, the subjective experience is an ambivalent one. The boy's anxiety arises out of a contradiction in the sexual experience: pride in the pleasure and power of the phallus but the simultaneous sense that the phallus is not really under his control.

The idea that the penis has a separate life is reflected in the tendency of young men to personify the penis by bestowing pet names upon it. Adolescent boys feel dread and shame at inopportune erections. One middle-aged man still described himself as being led around by his "joint." The young man's tragedy has been described as having a gun and ammunition, but no control. By the time control is achieved, the ammunition has been taken away. Wet dreams betray the boy's sexuality to his parents, particularly his mother. He feels he has no privacy.

Partly because self-control is crucial to mastery and partly out of gender training, control over his penis — and, through it, over the outside world — has high priority for the boy. Sexuality becomes imbued with issues of control and dominance. Yet the adolescent's sense of lack of control over the penis is never completely resolved. The lack of control becomes a locus for symbolic elaboration and is a key factor in shaping male fears about lack of conrol over the penis. It predisposes men to fears of impotence or premature ejaculation, the subjective evidence that they may not be fully in charge of their members.

Insecurity about his sexual adequacy and his ability to please the female are reinforced by another of the vagaries of sexual reality — a lifelong distinction between the sexes. Sexual excitement (or lack of it) is visible in only one.

How do men cope with these anxieties about performance and female rejection? Collectively and individually, men submerge their fears into an overestimation of male sexuality. Horney speculates, and I concur, that the boy's remedy for the narcissistic mortification implicit in the renunciation of his mother is a defensive phallic narcissism. Identification with the phallic father and his power, and subsequent identification with male sexual strength and independence, form the psychological core of the collective male ideal of male sexuality—macho sexuality. The boy's phallic narcissism, intensified by his adolescent pride in the erectile power of the penis, coalesces with the magical sexual properties with which he has endowed his father and other rivals. Out of this emerges the individual and collective male pride in some version of macho sexuality. (This solution is no doubt reinforced by male gender socialization, or "male bonding".)

Men attempt to assuage their sexual self-doubts through active sexuality (or fantasies of it), in which control over the penis is sought through sexual mastery and control over the sexual object. In his wishful fantasies, the male reverses his self-doubts and anxieties by endowing his penis with supernatural powers (those he once attributed to his all-powerful father).

The fear of female unavailability and rejection leads to compensatory fantasies featuring a cornucopia of sexually available women. We too often take fantasies of the omni-available woman and their enactments at face value, seen as requiring no further understanding. The male interest in multiple or simultaneous partners is accepted as part of his sexual voraciousness (rapaciousness?). These sexual enthusiasms, enter into the collective male ego ideal as part of an idealized macho sexuality. Yet there is something haunting in the fantasies—a denial and reversal of the realities of female sexuality, a magically exaggerated picture of male sexual prowess, and a wistful desire for a different sexual world. In fact, the male appears to project his own sexual desires onto his fantasy females. It is they who are forever randy, perpetually aroused and ready. Most important, they are always available and never reject him.

Fantasies of the omni-available woman reveal not only the pressing desire for female availability but the simultaneous desire to erase any one woman's individuality or importance. This obliteration provides reassurance about virility, the "on-call" availability of the sexual object, and the inherent importance of the man vis-á-vis a woman. While the fantasies may sometimes be contaminated by the need to discharge aggression, they are not fueled by it. These are not domination fantasies per se; they are more subtle, revealing the widespread need to bolster the male's subjective sense of control and command. They counter the dread of personal inadequacy, male subordination, and female rejection. The assumption is that women are automatically satisfied and require no special stimulation; they take their pleasure from his pleasure. But the fact that the omni-available female (even in fantasy) is often viewed with condescension, contempt, or even sadism is evidence of the resentment caused by the experience of frustration at the hands of the rejecting mother (and subsequent female objects).

Consequently, men may be internally driven to conquer women, to possess them, and to do so repeatedly. They may also split their sexual desires between a number of different women, usually those seen to be in an inferior position and therefore easily dominated. Men can thereby control the source of sexual gratification and insure the availability of one sexual object if another vanishes. In fantasy, it will be the woman, not the man, who is humiliated. It is she who will serve him, admire his penis, and submit.

Control of the sexual object serves as a compensatory device that defends against the male child's sense of inadequacy and inferiority vis-á-vis both parents and the humiliation of the unavailability of a sexual object at different points in his life. Out of revenge, the man reverses the humiliation implicit in both his infantile and his adolescent experience: he stands ready to demand sexual availability and fidelity while disavowing it for himself.

Normal Resolution Versus Power Resolution

I have suggested a series of developmental issues that are not intended as alternatives to the importance of castration anxiety in understanding male sexuality, but as factors that may modify the intensity of castration anxiety and interfere with its resolution. Intense and persistent castration anxiety can be the end result of a number of different contingent factors. One important factor, beyond the scope of this paper, is the strong female identification seen in some men, usually as a result of early separation anxiety (see, e.g., Ovesey & Person, 1973). Once it has developed, it may serve as an inhibitory force (one sees here the various forms of sexual inhibitions) or it may serve as a stimulus to a variety of reactive solutions, among these the development of a macho sexuality.

By and large, in normal development, castration anxiety, envy and fear of both parents, and the fear of female rejection will be largely resolved. However, even in "normal" male sexuality there will remain some latent or moderately active interest in multiple partners and Lesbian sex. In those instances in which there is failure of an adequate father identification or intense preoedipal rage (particularly directed against the mother), the (heterosexual) male has a propensity to develop a sexuality imbued with power concerns and preoccupations. These may easily revolve around sadomasochistic interactions and in extreme cases may find expression in sexual sadism, either fantasied or enacted. Consequently, it is probably accurate to say that the male tendency to sexual aggression and sadism has preoedipal roots related to the fact or fear of loss of the object or loss of love. But sadism ought not be considered the norm among men any more than masochism is viewed as the norm among women.

At the same time, there do appear to be specific problems inherent in male development that predispose to the centrality of concerns over control and power among the majority of men. The impulse to solve these problems through sexual domination grows out of the conviction that only possession and domination will guarantee fulfillment and give surcease to the endless wheel of desire. Ultimately the power of sexual domination is (mistakenly) invoked to preserve a precarious sense of self. This option is most readily invoked in any cultural milieu that glorifies such domination, that takes its apparent strength at face value, and minimizes its compensatory functions.

REFERENCES

Barclay, A. M. (1973). Sexual fantasies in men and women. *Medical Aspects of Human Sexuality*, 7:205-216.
Brenner, C. (1979). Depressive affect, anxiety, and psychic conflict in the phallic-oedipal phase. *Psychoanal. Q.*, 48:177-197.
Brownmiller, S. (1976). *Against Our Will: Men, Women and Rape*. New York: Bantam Books.
Chasseguet-Smirgel, J. (1984). *Creativity and Perversion*. New York: Norton.
Freud, S. (1920). Beyond the pleasure principle. *S.E.*, 18:7-64.
————— (1923). The infantile genital organization. *S.E.*, 19.
————— (1924). The economic problem in masochism. *S.E.*, 19:157-170.
Friday, N. (1980). *Men in Love: Male Sexual Fantasies: The Triumph of Love Over Rage*. New York: Delacourt.
Horney, K. (1932). The dread of women: Observations on a specific difference in the dread felt by men and women respectively for the opposite sex. *Int. J. Psychoanal.*, 13:348-360.
Kinsey, A. C., Pomeroy, W. B., Martin, C. E., & Gebhard, P. H. (1948). *Sexual Behavior in the Human Male*. Philadelphia: Saunders.
————— (1953). *Sexual Behavior in the Human Female*. Philadelphia & London: Saunders.
Lukianowicz, N. (1960). Imaginary sexual partner and visual masturbatory fantasies. *Arch. Gen. Psychiat.*, 3:429-449.
McDougall, J. (1980). *Plea for a Measure of Abnormality*. New York: Int. Univ. Press.
May, R. (1980). *Sex and Fantasy: Patterns of Male and Female Development*. New York: Norton.
Millett, K. (1970). *Sexual Politics*. Garden City, NY: Doubleday.
Ovesey, L. & Person, E. S. (1973). Gender identity and sexual psychopathology in men: A psychodynamic analysis of homosexuality, transsexualism, and transvestism. *J. Amer. Acad. Psychoanal.*, 2:53-72.
Person, E. S. (1985). Two fantasy preoccupations in men: The omni-available woman and Lesbian sex. Unpublished.
Person, E. S., Myers, W., Terestman, N., Goldberg, E., & Salvatore, C. (1983). Gender differences in sexual behaviors and sexual fantasies in a college population. Unpublished.
Thorne, E. (1971). *Your Erotic Fantasies*. New York: Ballantine Books.
van Lustbader, E. (1984). *The Miko*. New York: Villard Books.
Zilbergeld, B. (1978). *Male Sexuality*. New York: Bantam Books.

135 Central Park West
New York, N.Y. 10023

Nixon, Hitler, and Power: An Ego Psychological Study

PETER J. LOEWENBERG, Ph.D.

F REUD INITIATED THE ENTERPRISE we now call psychohistory not merely because he was a curious commentator, critic, and analyst of civilization who wished to present a "general psychology" that was valid for all mankind, and not merely because he was a deeply cultured man who would have preferred to be a philosopher rather than a clinician. He committed his psychodynamic ideas to the problems of history, culture, art, and literary criticism also as a strategy of presentation to circumvent the evidential problem of case histories. No one fully knows what goes on in any clinical psychoanalytic setting. Even in the Rat Man Case where we have Freud's notes, there is much that we must infer and will never know. Freud chose to demonstrate his insights and formulae of mental functioning by reference to the works of Leonardo and Michelangelo, Shakespeare, and Ibsen because these data and artifacts belong to the culture at large. Any person may obtain, study, scrutinize, and question Freud's interpretations from the same data base to see if they make sense or convey conviction. In their persistent quest for a more accurate model of the mind, Freud and his successors created models that reflected shifts in the culture at large; thus, the recent interest in narcissism.

Professor Loewenberg is a Professor of History, University of California, Los Angeles; member of the Faculty of the Southern California Psychoanalytic Institute. He is author of *Decoding the Past: The Psychohistorical Approach* (1985) and is an editor of the *Psychohistory Review*.

I will trace, as applied to history, what was a crucial move from libidinal drive models of psychology to the more recent use of ego psychological and object relations paradigms. The libido model has given us neat explanations of great force in biography. This model operates using the principles of repetition compulsion and the reenactment of trauma. It also has serious limitations, which must be recognized and may be improved upon in historical writing, just as the libido model has been updated in clinical psychoanalysis. My focus is on contemporary American historical research and writing on the exercise of power in the careers of Richard Nixon and Adolf Hitler; tracing the manipulations, successes, and reverses, in their quest for power, and their ultimate loss of power through their own destructive activity.

While there are several psychological biographies of Richard Nixon, including that by Bruce Mazlish (1972), who emphasizes early separation experiences, and Leo Rangell (1980), who sees a national failure of integrity, I choose to focus on the Fawn Brodie (1981) biography, which shows all the strengths and the flaws of an instinctual drive model for psychohistory. The model is one of great power and persuasiveness as one reads her account of the shaping of the character of the President whose tenure of office ended so ignobly with the exposure of his lies. One of Brodie's major themes is Nixon as a liar in matters large and small throughout his life. She contends that "Nixon lied to gain love, to store up his grandiose fantasies, to bolster his ever-wavering sense of identity. He lied in attacks, hoping to win . . . And always he lied, and this most aggressively, to deny that he lied . . . Finally, he enjoyed lying" (Brodie, 1981, p. 25). She shows Nixon lying about such trivia as his college major, his wife's first name and birthdate, as well as in his first campaign for Congress against incumbent Jerry Voorhis; about his secret slush fund in the 1952 Presidential campaign, and, of course, in the Watergate cover-up. Brodie structures an argument that Nixon learned to lie in boyhood from a "myth-making mother" who denied what was uncomfortable and stretched the truth, and from a brutal, hot-tempered father who punished his boys with the strap and rod when he failed to get instant obedience, and that Richard learned to be, in his words, "pretty convincing to avoid punishment." She argues that "almost every one of Nixon's victories and political achievements save the elections to the vice-presidency has been won as a result of lying attack or the unexpected and fortuitious death of others" (p. 507). Her emphasis on the theme of Nixon the liar from boyhood to maturity, from parental home to the White House, is essentially static and while powerful is unbalanced in its neglect of Nixon's many ego strengths and adaptations in a long political career.

I suggest the psychohistorian must look carefully at the vicissitudes of Nixon's ego functioning in the dimensions of time and circumstance in order to gain a richer, more nuanced, more accurate portrait of the man. By "ego functions" I mean the part of Nixon's mind that dealt with reality: coped with stress and defeat, found modes of adapting to new and unforeseen situations, made assessments concerning the future, evaluated inputs of information, and distinguished — or failed to discern — facts from his own wishes. The use of ego psychology in history suggests that we look carefully and time-specifically at where Nixon effectively tested reality and when and where he did not; when he adapted successfully to stresses and set backs and when he did not. In short, those areas and times when his personality broke down or functioned most effectively will tell us much about the make-up and patterning of his defense mechanisms, which was his character. This model and method is supremely historical because it is preeminently time-specific — always posing the question: "Why now?"

An ego psychological view would look at how skillfully and cleverly during all of his career — until the end when he had reached the pinnacle of political power — Nixon knew and supplied exactly what the American public wished to hear. He was a vicious anti-Communist "gut fighter" in his campaigns against Jerry Voorhis in 1946 and Helen Gahagan Douglas in 1950, and in his investigation of the Alger Hiss case. I emphasize this not to endorse his witch-hunting, but merely to say he knew what the public wanted to hear. He sensed the mood of the electorate and ruthlessly exploited it. Years later sensing that Americans were prepared to tolerate the recognition of Communist China and detente with the Russians, Nixon eagerly led the way. I also think a President deserves credit for discernment and talent in his appointments and that Nixon's choice of Henry Kissinger to steer American foreign policy was of a high order.

In the 1952 Presidential campaign, Nixon saved his political career and the Republican ticket with his maudlin "Checkers" speech. General Eisenhower was ready to drop him from the GOP slate. His career appeared to be finished. We may listen to the speech today and find the emotional tone unctuous and revolting, but at that time he knew what would sell and he produced it. He always remained within the boundaries of the law. He had, as Brodie puts it, "the skill of a man who can profit successfully on the fringes of political graft" (1981, p. 280).

A man who could repeatedly transform major defeats into mere setbacks, as Nixon did, gives evidence of great ego strength. He lost the race for the Presidency to Kennedy in 1960. Two years later he could not even win the Governorship of California, his home state. By any expectable evaluation of political prospects in America, his career was again finally finished. Yet he traveled the country and rebuilt the power of a Republican Party riven by vituperative conflict between Rockefeller and Goldwater factions; he mended political fences and emerged as the leader of choice to win the Presidency he had so long sought.

The psychohistorical problem of Nixon and Watergate then is not why he was a liar, rather, it is a question of timing — that most critical historical and psychological question: "Why did he destroy his power now?" He had achieved his life aim. He was an experienced lawyer, a veteran of both the House and Senate, an accomplished Congressional investigator. One has to be highly provocative to bring the Congress to draft a resolution of impeachment, truly the gravest of political rejections our constitutional system allows. One must be so provocative as to give the congressional committee two pieces of evidence, such as a tape and a transcript, that do not match. To have brought events to the pass of political isolation and national demoralization that Nixon achieved requires great unconscious effort and poor reality testing. It demanded that he be profligate with regard to his political advantages and largely alienate the political and opinion-making sectors of society, including those of his own party, which desire to respond positively to the awe and the power the office of President of the United States confers. The psychohistorical question for research is why did this most cunning of politicians show such poor judgment and reality testing, which was generally uncharacteristic of him, *at that time*, not all of his prevaricating life.

When putting this question, the psychohistorian will be led to the interesting answer that Nixon created his own failure of power in the Watergate Affair precisely at the pinnacle of his success — after having achieved re-election to the Presidency by one of the greatest popular margins in American history. This is a pattern of unconscious ambivalence and guilt about power first delineated in Freud's 1916 essay, "Those Wrecked by Success." Nixon apparently unconsciously needed to fail in order to appease his guilt. His political destruction was his own work and his alone. Nixon turned his triumph into dust, destroying a power of which he unconsciously felt unworthy.

Psychological interpretations have appropriately taken a leading place in the continuing attempts to understand the Nazi Movement, the Third Reich, and the person of Adolf Hitler. The current literature provides an excellent forum in which to survey the state of applications of psychology to history on the issue of power. The three conceptual areas in which a knowledge and use of psychodynamics will make a substantial difference in historical formulation and conclusions are in the application of ego psychology, in taking most seriously and interpreting psychoanalytically Hitler's fantasies, and in the utilization of the varieties of psychoanalytic object relations theory. In examining these problems, we cannot only arrive at an assessment of Hitler's use of power, but we may also come to some conclusions regarding the state and method of psychohistorical writing today and venture some answers as to what psychoanalytic psychology can and cannot do for history.

An early strand of Hitler scholarship puts the spotlight on his destructiveness and self-destructiveness but without the time-specific
developmental dimension that is the essence of both historical and
clinical work. McRandle (1965), in a suggestive essay, lifts out the
many depressed and suicidal aspects of Hitler's career. McRandle
finds in Hitler "a tendency to fail in everything he attempted. He
failed at school, he failed as an artist, and he failed in his relationships with other human beings. Furthermore, there is at least some
reason to believe that these failures were self-induced" (p. 156).
McRandle points to Hitler's youthful suicide threats as one example
of a self-destructive tendency demonstrating that "between 1900
and 1914 Hitler acted in such a manner to insure his continued failure" (p. 169). McRandle cogently poses the psychological problem
of explanation: "It is amazing that a person who had failed so consistently in the endeavors of the first half of his life should be so as-
toundingly successful in the following years" (1965, p. 170). The
relevant issue is not the presence of failures, for all men and all parties have failed at some junctures. What must be assessed is how
Hitler coped with defects and twists of fortune, when and where he
surmounted them and was able to use them to his own and his
movement's benefit.

Erich Fromm (1973), writing about human destructiveness, finds
Hitler the prime example of a "necrophilous character," by which
he means a person dedicated to the destruction of life. Fromm believes this was caused by Hitler's malignant incestuous early relationship with his mother. Certainly Hitler is one of the most destructive, morbid, deadly, and death-oriented figures in history.
The proof that he was so is there in his actions in the historical record. But what is gained by taking this proof and tautologically giv-
ing it the labels "necrophilous" and "malignant aggression?"
Fromm's circular hypothesis tells us nothing about Hitler we do not
already know. What we need to know is precisely *when* Hitler was
politically competent and when he was disaster-prone in terms of
political functioning.

Another interpretation is offered by Binion (1976), who proposes
an absolute psychic determination of the repetition of a presumed

youthful trauma. At age 18, according to Binion's reconstruction, Hitler's mother was given an overdose of iodoform gauze and prematurely killed by a Jewish doctor, Eduard Bloch, who was treating her for breast cancer. From here Binion moves to Hitler's trauma from mustard-gas poisoning in the First World War. Thus, Binion writes of Hitler's exposure to mustard gas on the Western Front in 1918: "When it condensed on his skin Hitler associated it with Bloch's iodoform. But then he expanded it to associate it with asphyxiating gas as well. The gas chambers resulted" (1976, p. 131). This kind of reductionism relies on a pre-ego psychological level of psychodynamics.

Waite's (1977) study of Hitler is in a broader historical context, yet takes account of the power of fantasy and treats evidence with psychoanalytic perceptiveness. For example, his inference that Hitler had a primal-scene trauma is based on the careful reconstruction of Hitler's self-reference from his fantasied reports of brutal assault by father and rape of the mother observed by a hypothetical three-year-old boy. The case is convincing because of an overwhelming convergence of fantasied events with the data of Hitler's childhood. Waite is most pertinently psychoanalytic when he says: "We shall never know with finality whether the infant Adolf actually saw the scene of sexual assault. But in his fantasy he did, and it was for him a 'primal scene trauma' " (1977, p. 162.)[1]

Stierlin (1975), taking an approach to Hitler based on his clinical work with families, postulates a generational dynamic in which Hitler served as the "delegated" agent of his mother to remain psychologically deeply dependent on her, to be living evidence of her good mothering, to give glory, excitement, and importance to her life, and to be her avenger and ally against a husband who neglected and oppressed her. Stierlin draws out the psychological implications of Hitler's "Petronella" story (see Trevor-Roper, 1961, p. 201), which describes how his Steyr landlady humiliated her hus-

---

[1] Waite's interpretation of these beating fantasies draws on the strongest part of the 1943 psychoanalytic study of Hitler prepared for the U.S. Office of Strategic Services (see Langer, 1972, pp. 141–145).

band by locking him out of the house overnight until he was readmitted in the morning, cowed and pitiful. Hitler tells of his own refusal to unbolt the door to the pleading man and that he despised the husband as a "wet rag." Stierlin asks, why did Hitler take the part of the wife and not the husband? He suggests the answer lies in Hitler's relation to his mother, who comforted him when his father beat him, and whom he felt was a loyal ally. Thus, he avenges her in fantasy and lets her triumph over the husband whom he pictures as a ridiculous weakling. Stierlin lacks historical evidence for his general thesis of maternal "delegation," but when he deals with Hitler's own fantasies as a raconteur and his identifications in sadistic humor, we have evidence of true internalization deriving from relations with his mother. We can see his mother as he saw her — a powerful object introjected to become a part of him.

When all these identifications are demonstrated, it is still a historically static picture of Hitler. I concur with the thrust of George Mosse's critique (1976, p. 506) of psychological treatments of Hitler:

> I remain puzzled why psychohistory persists in concentrating on one side of Hitler's character, namely his youth and adolescence and his supposed abnormalities and neuroses. It is difficult to see from this approach how his political genius was formed as well as the source of his superb sense of timing and his ability to learn from past mistakes . . . . Why not call a moratorium on analyses of this side of his character (which certainly may have existed) and instead study the personality factor behind his actions which in fact made him one of the most successful statesmen of our century?

In order to meet Mosse's challenge, historians need to add ego psychology to our research armamentarium.

To demonstrate the congruence of psychoanalytic ego psychology with historical method, let us examine Hitler in action to determine precisely when his ego functions of reality testing and adaptation in specific foreign and domestic areas worked well and when they broke down and failed. To this end let us examine Hitler's functioning in three particular moments in history: (1) the party crisis after the failure of the Munich *Putsch*, 1923–1925; (2) the period of electoral decline in the party's fortunes in the fall and winter of 1932; (3) the series of diplomatic and military errors and miscalculations beginning with Dunkirk in 1940, culminating in the declaration of war against the United States in December, 1941, and including close attention to the decision-making on the Eastern front at the Battles of Kiev and Stalingrad.

We are immediately struck by Hitler's skill at holding the reins of leadership even after the debacle of the 1923 Munich *Putsch*. Hitler was in prison and contending leaders were fighting for the succession. He categorically refused to intervene in their quarrels. His silence encouraged their divisive feuding. Orlow (1969, p. 51) writes: "When Hitler emerged from his prison cell in December, he returned as a saint, eagerly awaited and welcomed by all of the volkisch groups." His first speech upon his release was "a masterful effort" (p. 54). Gordon (1972, p. 618) evaluates Hitler's ego functioning in the period after the *Putsch* thus: "It was here, in the months after the Putsch, that one finds the real Triumph des Willens. By sheer determination and sense of mission Hitler transformed himself from the frenetic revolutionary who had been shattered and silenced by the Putsch into a political leader ready to accept years of careful building and constant struggle as a prelude to power."

Hitler had an extraordinary ability to understand and make use of the weakness of his opponents. Within the party he knew how to divide them and strike them one by one. In Orlow's (1969) estimation he met the left-wing challenge of Gregor Strasser in 1925 "brilliantly." He coped with a major challenge by the northern leaders of the party by staging a meeting in his stronghold of Bamberg in February, 1926. He seduced Goebbels, the only major northern figure he had not won over. He invited Goebbels to Munich in early April to address a mass rally, lent him his car, and gave him a personal tour of party headquarters. After this treatment Goebbels was "putty in Hitler's hands." Goebbels wrote in his diary on April 13, 1926, "Hitler is a great man. He forgives us and shakes our hand. Let us forget the past" (Orlow, 1969, p. 72).

The greatest test of the sureness of Hitler's leadership came in the fall of 1932. The Nazis had done sensationally well in the July 31, 1932 Reichstag elections, more than doubling their vote of 1930, from 6.4 million to 13.7 million. Their Reichstag seats jumped from 107 to 230, making theirs by far the largest party. There was, however, a feeling of exhaustion, a sense that time was the party's enemy. Subscriptions to party newspapers began to drop off in the fall of 1932. In some *Gaus*[2] the number of resignations exceeded applications for membership. The debts from the July election had not been paid. The party's finances were severely strained. It was difficult to raise the new campaign contributions for the fourth national campaign within a year. Local elections were going against the NSDAP. In a local election in East Prussia on October 9, 1932, the Nazi vote which had been 1,074 in Konigsberg in July dropped to 483, in Gerdauen it also dropped from 1,074 to 126 (Orlow, 1969, pp. 284, 288–289).

In the November 6, 1932 Reichstag elections the Nazis suffered severe setbacks in all areas of Germany. No *Gau* was able to maintain its July strength. Nationally, the vote dropped from 13.7 million to 11.7 million in November and the number of seats in the Reichstag fell from 230 to 196. It appeared that the strategy of massive electoral victories had come to a dead end and that the Nazi drive for power had peaked in July, 1932. Strasser put Hitler under pressure to join a coalition with the argument that the National Socialist wave had crested. Hitler stood firm, refusing to join any government not headed by himself and having extensive decree powers. He refused to settle for partial power or a partial victory. The pressure on him was intense. Membership increases declined sharply. *Gau* Brandenburg suffered a net membership decline in November. Party finances were regarded as "hopeless." Local elections in Saxony on November 14 and in Thuringia on December 3 showed disastrous losses in both areas. "In this circumstance," writes Allan Bullock, "it was only Hitler's determination and leadership that kept the Party going. His confidence in himself never wavered.

---

[2]The *Gau* was a National Socialist party district.

When the Gauleiters assembled at Munich in early October he used all his arts to put new life and energy into them" (1961, p. 191). Reichschancellor Schliecher sought to use the crisis in the party and the pressure on Hitler by offering him a Vice Chancellorship, and the posts of Prussian Prime Minister and Minister of the Interior for other Nazis. Hitler remained adamant. Despite his own and his associates' "hunger for power," and the severe electoral setbacks, Hitler categorically refused all compromises or offers of coalition. In Orlow's words (1969), "The NSDAP at the end of 1932 was well on its way to the rubbish pile of history" (pp. 290, 308). Yet, as we know, history turned out otherwise. And in this case, at this particular time, it was Hitler's adaptation to the political realities of Germany and his capacity to deal with great inner and outer stress that took him to power on his own terms on January 30, 1933. If, as Bullock so memorably notes, "Hitler did not seize power; he was jobbed into office by a backstairs intrigue" (1961, p. 213), we must acknowledge his skill and effectiveness at dealing with such masters of intrigue as Franz von Papen and General Kurt von Schleicher. He understood the unscrupulous political power game at the end of Weimar better than his counterplayers.

One of the earliest and most original interpretations of Hitler and his relation to the German people is that of Erik H. Erikson (1963). In a formulation that has now become a classic, he interprets Hitler's *Mein Kampf* as a myth made by the man himself, a legend of a hard and bitter youth, a harsh tyrannical civil servant father and a devoted, loving mother. Hitler pictures himself as a talented, sensitive son who wanted to be an artist and who refused to submit to his father's desire to make him a Habsburg civil servant, a good orderly bourgeois. He refused to identify with his father. Erikson said:

Psychologists overdo the father attributes in Hitler's historical image; Hitler the adolescent who refused to become a father by any connotation, or for that matter, a kaiser or a president. He did not repeat Napoleon's error. He was the Führer: A glorified older brother, ... he reserved for himself the new position of

the one who remains young in possession of supreme power. He
was the unbroken adolescent . . . . a gang leader who kept the
boys together by demanding their admiration, by creating terror,
and by shrewdly involving them in crimes from which there was
no way back [pp. 336–337].

What, we may ask, is the meaning of Erikson's famous interpretation of Hitler that: "This combination of personal revelation and
shrewd propaganda (together with loud and determined action) at
last carried with it that universal conviction for which the smol-
dering rebellion in German youth had been waiting. . . . Both father and sons could now identify with the Führer, an adolescent
who never gave in" (Erikson, 1973, p. 337)? What is implied is what
I wish to explicitly delineate here—to have unconsciously constructed a myth with such a widespread appeal to German youth
and adults is a major feat of synthesis, creativity, and adaptation.
Most of us do not even know what is going on with contemporary
youth, let alone have the ability to appeal to them in a political
movement. Here, two of the points I wish to make come together:
Hitler's ability to use his fantasies and to adapt them to the political
purpose of building a movement with a mass following and how
Hitler's fantasies led to his own and the Third Reich's destruction.
     A recent expression of an old thesis is given by Stern (1975) and
Heer (1968), who see Nazism as a secularized religion, particularly
an aberrant form of Roman Catholicism, and Hitler as its psychologically sensitive prophet. Hitler's program was successful, says
Stern, because it was "conducted under the image in the language of
transcendence, as the answer to a religious longing and demand" (p.
97). Hitler's communion, according to Heer (1968), was *Volks-
gemeinschaft* (community of the people); his ritual, mass meetings;
his Mass, the celebration of the sacred Great War (p. 184). There is
more than a little truth here. Religion expresses the mystical and unconscious needs of its communicants. Repressed by the rationalist
science of the nineteenth century which reached its high point in
Germany, the unconscious revenged itself in varieties of pseudo-
religions, among them *Völkisch* sects and National Socialism.

The founders of religions are often under the sway of delusions, megalomania, and psychotic ideation, as Fawn Brodie (1960) has shown in her study of Joseph Smith. To present to the world a set of fantasies that induce in others a need to share them and to become followers is not necessarily a sign of sanity, but it is the sign of a good salesman. Certain kinds of sociopaths are notorious for their ability to sell with conviction, to lie, and to feel no guilt.

Hitler was flexible on all political issues to the point of being totally unprincipled. He succeeded in accommodating to the churches, including the Vatican in the Concordat of July 20, 1933, which recognized the right of the Roman Catholic Church in Germany to manage is own affairs. On the issue of socialization, he succeeded in neutralizing the party's left wing and appealed to Germany's industrialists for support. He manipulated Reichswehr Generals, whom he at first needed, into supporting him in 1934, and then managed to control them and force them into subservience in 1938.

When we turn to the war itself and the spring of 1940 we begin to find the commission of a series of failures, miscalculations, and finally self-destructive acts by Hitler in startling contrast to his prior acute judgment, flexibility, and sense of the possible. In the Norwegian campaign, Hitler was prepared to withdraw when the British made a decisive naval strike in Narvik fjord. Hitler, notes Chief of the General Staff, Franz Halder (1950), "was completely at a loss at the appearance of the first major crisis at Narvik, and but for the energetic intervention of his senior military adviser in Supreme Headquarters would have called off the whole operation" (p. 32).

Hitler's subsequent failure to follow up the Ardennes breakthrough in the Western offensive of May, 1940 was a major puzzle to military contemporaries and is still a point of controversy among historians. On May 24 Guderian's tanks, which were part of von Kleist's army group, were at Gravelines on the River Aa, 12 miles west of Dunkirk and in position to capture the last channel port of escape open to the British Expeditionary Force. The British headquarters was 42 miles to the southeast at Lille, thus the German panzers were 30 miles closer to Dunkirk than most of the British armies. At noon on May 24 Hitler, agreeing with Rundstedt's advice, issued a "Tank Halt" order that stopped his panzers for three days. Rundstedt's motives were his concern that the western wing of the German advance was too weak to withstand a possible Anglo-French thrust from the south and he wished to conserve armored strength for an anticipated main battle in France.

Hitler allowed Göring to persuade him that the "National Socialist Luftwaffe" rather than the "conservative-traditional" army could alone destroy the surrounded Allied armies. To the German army would merely remain the task of occupying the territory. On the evening of May 24 the Luftwaffe was given the assignment of "breaking all enemy resistance in the encircled area, and to prevent the escape of English forces across the Channel" (Jacobsen, 1960, p. 121). The army leadership in the field was distressed and protested the "Tank Halt" order, to no avail. In his postwar memoirs Guderian (1951) writes: "We were stopped within sight of Dunkirk! We saw the German air attacks. But we also saw the small and large ships of every kind with which the English left the fortress" (pp. 105–106). The British Expeditionary Force and their French allies were, owing to this series of miscalculations, able to stage the dramatic retreat by sea which has made "Dunkirk" synonymous with seizing moral victory from the specter of annihilation. In the scales of history, notes Ansel:

> Hitler relinquished physical contact with his most dangerous foe on the field of battle at the crucial moment, and thereby he loosened his grip on the operational initiative and likewise the political. This became the eventual result of the Tank Halt Order. . . . (a) flagrant blunder in war making [which] gambled that priceless military advantage, the operational initiative on the ground, for dubious psychopolitical effect, and . . . . lost [1960, pp. 89–90].

Nor did Hitler follow through with an invasion of England in the summer and fall of 1940. The reason is that Hitler was ambivalent in the extreme about England, wishing both to destroy her and gain her as an ally. He was indecisive, he obsessed, he kept pushing the date of invasion back, he placed the *Luftwaffe's* securing of air superiority as a condition precedent to "Operation Sea Lion." Hitler hoped, all evidence to the contrary, that England would sue for peace. The extent of his ambivalence is evident when we look at the wording of the first two sentences of his *Directive No. 16* of July 16, 1940, "On Preparations for a Landing Operation Against England":

Since England, in spite of her hopeless military situation, shows no signs of being ready to come to an understanding, I have decided to prepare a landing operation against England and, *if necessary*, to carry it out.

The aim of this operation will be to eliminate the English homeland as a base for the prosecution of the war against Germany and, *if necessary*, to occupy it completely [Trevor-Roper, 1964, p. 34, emphasis added].

Geoffrey C. Cocks (1977) points out that the repeated phrase, "if necessary," indicated Hitler's hope that it would not be necessary. Says Ansel: "Invasion England failed to happen, not because Hitler willed against it, but because he could not will at all where she was concerned!" He concludes: "More than any other single factor Adolf Hitler rendered invasion impossible" (1960, pp. 316, 321).

Waite (1981) focuses on Hitler's decision-making in 1941 and 1942, analyzing three decisions he believes "cry out for psychological assistance": (1) the decision to invade Russia in June, 1941; (2) his declaration of war on the United States in December, 1941, and (3) his order to kill all of Europe's Jews from 1942 to 1945. Waite has located the general turning point of Hitler's failure to perceive and adapt to reality in the early war period. Although I think the events of 1940, at the height of his success, already presage the coming series of failures in reality testing and in decision-making, Waite's ego psychological approach of carefully examining Hitler's coping at time-specific crises and turning points is congruent with good historical method and should also be applied to the earlier period of the twenties and thirties.

When we look at the disasters of the Russian campaign there are a number of points and decisions where, notwithstanding the pervasive postwar efforts of his generals to place all blame on Hitler's doorstep, the judgment of the Führer may be considered calamitous for the German armies. Among these disastrous junctures are certainly Hitler's insistence on an early victory at Kiev rather than pushing toward Moscow, the central point of Soviet power, until the autumn mud slowed the advance into Russia.

The catastrophe of military catastrophes for the German armies in the Second World War, the *ne plus ultra* of German advance and disaster was, of course, the battle of Stalingrad. It is here that Hitler on November 24, 1942, forbade the surrounded 6th Army to break out of its encirclement. General von Paulus faithfully obeyed his Führer's orders not to withdraw, and he did not attempt to meet from within the encirclement the rescue attempts of Field Marshall von Manstein's Army Group Don from the southwest. We can concur with Hans-Adolf Jacobsen's finding that: "There is no doubt . . . that Hitler, as Commander-in-Chief of the Wehrmacht and Supreme Commander of the Army, bears the greatest share of responsibility for this severe political and military catastrophe in the winter of 1942–1943" (1967, pp. 147–149).

Once again Hitler chose to trust Göring's promises that he could supply the beleaguered army at Stalingrad by air, although a few minutes' calculation would have indicated that this was an empty boast. By contrast, according to Schramm (1971), in the summer of 1944 Hitler was able to set up complex calculations "on a moment's notice" of how far inland Allied ships off the coast would be able to reach with their fire, including variables of the different depths of offshore waters, and the differences in the caliber of naval guns. We may ask why this virtuousity with technical details was unavailable to him a year and a half earlier at Stalingrad, and why he chose to believe Göring's grandiose claims for the second time.

Hitler's sense of timing in foreign policy was excellent in the 1930s. He knew exactly how to handle to his advantage the likes of

Edouard Daladier, Neville Chamberlain, and the Polish colonels. However, when we turn to the diplomatic history of World War II, we find that the fine sensibility of the thirties is no longer there. We see the effective step by step destruction of his power. To take only one example, Hitler's policy toward the United States was a demonstration of impulsive, self-defeating behavior. I here follow Norman Rich (1973), who carefully considers the motivations for Hitler's precipitous declaration of war on the United States on December 11, 1941. Rich asks why Hitler did not procrastinate, maneuver for all the time he could get, before enlisting another enemy at the very time he was hard pressed in the Battle of Moscow. Rich points out that Hitler did not even exact the price of Japanese support against Russia. Rich's logic is as forceful and rational as Hitler's strategy was irrational:

Hitler's declaration of war on the United States [was] an act which brought Germany no appreciable military or economic advantages and one which cancelled out the greatest benefit to Germany of the Japanese attack, namely its diversion of American attention from Europe to the Pacific. Once Japan had committed itself to war with the United States and all danger of a Japanese-American rapproachment had been removed, Hitler might surely have found excuses to procrastinate about fulfilling his pledge to join Japan in that war. At the very least he might have demanded Japanese support against Russia in turn for German support against America, if only a promise to stop American shipments to Russia via Vladivostok [p. 237].

We may well subscribe to Rich's finding that Hitler's war against the United States was an unnecessarily self-destructive act: "By declaring war on America while the greater part of his army was still bogged down in Russia, Hitler sealed his fate, and for that reason alone this action must be considered the greatest single mistake of his career" (Rich, 1973, p. 245).[3]

---

[3]The feelings of irritation conveyed in these citations should itself be a clue to subsequent historians that we are on the ground of irrationality in action.

An ego psychological approach may be integrated with object relation insights into personality. Ego psychology deals with the
adaptation to reality, while object relations tell us about the subject's inner world. It is here that facile notions concerning "reality"
must be put in relation to the indispensable moral dimension: effective and adaptative for which purpose and to what end?

When we probe Hitler's words and writings for the fantasy that
dominates his unconscious, we invariably come to the immutable
presence of the Jew. There is a letter of Hitler's from as early as September, 1919 calling for "the removal of Jews" (*die Entfernung der
Juden*) (Deuerlein, 1969, p. 47; Jackel, 1969, p. 60). This is the
earliest written document of Hitler's political engagement. The Jew
remained his primary fantasied enemy in his fight for German, Eu-
ropean, and eventually world power. According to Rauschning
(1940, p. 223),[4] Hitler said: "The struggle for world domination will
be fought out only between us two, between Germans and Jews. All
else is a false façade. Behind England stands Israel, behind France,
and behind the USA. Even when we have driven the Jew out of
Germany, he will still remain our world enemy."

If the Jew did not exist, said Hitler, "then we would have to invent
him. We need a visible enemy, not just an intangible one" (*Dann
mussten wir ihn erfinden. Man braucht einen Sichtbaren Feind,
nicht bloss einen unsichtbaren*). But Hitler seems to have realized
that placing the enemy outside himself was a defense, that the real
enemy lay within: *Der Jude sitzt immer in uns* (Rauschning, 1940,
p. 223). How else can we read this statement? As Friedrich Heer
(1968, p. 301) says, it sounds as if it had been made by a Freudian
psychoanalyst rather than by Adolf Hitler. "But," Hitler goes on,
"it is easier to fight him embodied as a person than as an invisible
demon" (*Aber es ist leichter ihn in leiblicher Gestalt zu bekampfen,
als den unsichtbaren Damon*) (Rauschning, 1940, p. 223).

For Hitler, the Jew was omnipresent and omnipotent. Anti-
Semitism was central to his ideology and an inflexible part of his po-

---

[4]Schieder (1972) carefully assessed and weighed the value of these reports for the period
1932–1934 and found them a unique and irreplaceable documentary source.

litical program and rhetoric. This distinguishes hatred of Jews from all other tenets of the Hitlerian faith such as anticapitalism, anti-Bolshevism, anti-Junkerism, anti-Slav, or anti-Anglicism. Hitler's anti-Semitism was of a psychotic quality. all lustful, evil, and sadistic parts of himself were projected onto the Jews. He remained pure, good, and righteous. The Jews were a projection of split off "bad" feelings about himself. He had to get these feelings away from himself and out to where they could be destroyed. Hence the paranoid defense — the badness is someplace else; hence, too, the extreme character of both his sadistic and his constructive fantasies. His persecutors were awesomely frightful and his idealized "good" parts were perfect. In the period after 1940 the Jews, having been neutralized and then destroyed, could no longer serve as an external source of danger. Hitler now megalomaniacally turned his paranoia to foreign targets: the Soviet Union and the United States. He used an omnipotent mania to control and master his inner badness. From June to December, 1941, he "suffered from an agonizing heart condition, attacks of dizziness, constant stomach ache, and debilitating bouts of shivering" (Maser, 1973, p. 160). Hitler thought he had stomach cancer and that he was in a race with death. Since 1936, he had been under treatment by a medical quack and had received daily injections of dextrose, hormones, and vitamins. He also received increasing dosages of stimulants such as amphetamines and barbituates, "Dr. Koster's Antigas-Pillen" which included strychnine and belladonna (Röhrs, 1966, pp. 73-74, 79-80, 118).

Hitler's thoughts in December, 1941 turned to inner decay and death, which he associated with the Jews. According to a stenographic record, Hitler said,

Many Jews were not aware of the destructive character of their existence. But, he who destroys life chooses death for himself, and they do not deserve any better. . . . . Their deeds produce the reaction. This follows action, as the bacillus succeeds the body it has killed!

One can be shocked by the way creatures devour each other in nature. The fly is killed by the dragon-fly, which is killed by a bird, which in turn is killed by a larger one. The largest creature, when it grows old, falls prey to bacteria. And finally, in another manner these also find their fate [Picker, 1965, pp. 152–153].

The badness and decay was close to home—in his stomach. His defense was megalomania—he could do anything, he could take on the whole world. On December 19, 1941, he dismissed General Brauchitsch and announced he would take over the command-in-chief of the German Army in the field. On January 30, 1942, Hitler spoke of his "unbounded confidence in myself, so that nothing, whatever it may be, can throw me out of the saddle, so that nothing can shake me." Bullock (1961) comments that "supremely confident in his powers, Hitler did not stop to reflect that, in his new position, it would be less easy to find scapegoats in the future" (pp. 601, 602). His judgment was now impaired by grandiosity and defensive manic omnipotence in order to combat the fears of deterioration and disintegration from within.

Both Nixon and Hitler followed undistinguished early years with rises to power culminating in the achievement of their inordinate ambitions. Both showed an extraordinary capacity for adaptation as they climbed the ladder to success. Both seemed to have lost this capacity when everything they sought was within their grasp. Both saw to their own destruction. When Nixon reached the apex of his power, he destroyed it at Watergate. Hitler, who had a degree of domestic power in Germany unknown to previous tyrants because it was abetted by modern methods of communications, pushed beyond the limits of his power and crafted his own and the Third Reich's destruction.

I have rehearsed historical facts to account for the time-specific ego functioning of these two twentieth-century leaders of differing polities, one a democracy, the other a totalitarian state, in order to provide the first step in answer to the psychoanalytical and historical question, "Why now?"

REFERENCES

Ansell, W. (1960). *Hitler Confronts England*. Durham, North Carolina: Duke Univ. Press.
Binion, R. (1976). *Hitler Among the Germans*. New York: Elsevier.

Brodie, F. M. (1960). *No Man Knows My History: The Life of Joseph Smith, The Mormon Phophet.* New York: Knopf.

_____ (1981). *Richard Nixon: The Shaping of His Character.* New York: Norton.

Bullock, A. (1961). *Hitler: A Study in Tyranny,* rev. ed. New York: Harper & Row.

Cocks, G. (1977). Comment on Binion. *Psychohistory Rev.,* 6(1):64–71.

Deuerlein, E. (1969). *Hitler: Eine politische Biographie.* Munich: P. List.

Erikson, E. (1963). *Childhood and Society,* 2nd ed. New York: Norton.

Freud, S. (1916). Some character-types met with in psychoanalytic work. *S.E.,* 14.

Fromm, E. (1973). *The Anatomy of Human Destructiveness.* New York: Holt, Rinehart, & Winston.

Gordon, H., Jr. (1972). *Hitler and the Beer Hall Putsch.* Princeton, N.J.: Princeton Univ. Press.

Guderian, H. (1951). *Erinnerungen eines Soldaten.* Heidelberg: Vowinckel.

Halder, F. (1950). *Hitler as War Lord,* trans. Paul Findlay. London: Putnam.

Heer, F. (1968). *Der Glaube des Adolf Hitler: Anatomie einer Politischen Religiösität.* Munich: Bechtle.

Jäckel, E. (1969). *Hitlers Weltanschauung: Entwurf einer Herrschaft.* Tübingen: Rainer Wunderlich Verlag Hermann Leins.

Jacobsen, H.-A. (1960). *Dokumente zum Westfeldzug 1940.* Göttingen: Musterschmidt.

_____ (1967). Zur schlacht von Stalingrad. In *Probleme des Zweiten Weltkrieges,* ed. Andreas Hillgruber. Koln: V. Kiepenheuer & Witsch., pp. 147–149.

Langer, W. C. (1972). *The Mind of Adolf Hitler: The Secret Wartime Report.* New York: Basic Books.

McRandle, J. (1965). The suicide. In *The Track of the Wolf: Essays on National Socialism and Its Leader, Adolf Hitler.* Evanston, Il.: Northwestern Univ. Press, pp. 146–248.

Maser, W. (1973). *Hitler: Legend, Myth, and Reality,* trans. P. & B. Ross. New York: Harper & Row.

Mazlish, B. (1972). *In Search of Nixon.* New York: Basic Books.

Mosse, G. L. (1976). Comment on Stierlin. *History of Childhood Q.,* 3(4):505–507.

Orlow, D. (1969). *The History of the Nazi Party: 1919–1933.* Pittsburgh: Univ. Pittsburgh Press.

Picker, H. (1965). *Hitlers Tischgespräche im Führerhauptquartier, 1941–1942.* 2nd ed. Stuttgart: Seewald Verlag.

Rangell, L. (1980). *The Mind of Watergate.* New York: Norton.

Rauschning, H. (1940). *Gespräche mit Hitler.* New York: Europa Verlag.

Rich, N. (1973). *Hitler's War Aims, Ideology, the Nazi State, and the Course of Expansion,* vol. I. New York: Norton.

Röhrs, H-D. (1966). *Hitler's Krankheit: Tatsachen und Legenden: Medizinische und psychische Grundlagen seines Zusammenbruchs.* Neckargemund: V. Vowinckel.

Schieder, T. (1972). Hermann Rauschning's 'Gespräche mit Hitler als Geschichtesquelle, *Rheinisch-Westfalische Akademie der Wissenschaften,* Vortrage G: 173 (Opladen).

Schramm, P. (1971). *Hitler: The Man and the Military Leader,* trans. & ed. D. S. Detwiler. Chicago: Quadrangle Books

Stern, J. P. (1975). *Hitler: The Führer and the People.* Berkeley & Los Angeles: Univ. California Press.

Stierlin, H. (1975). *Adolf Hitler: Familien Perspektiven.* Frankfurt am Main: Suhrkamp Verlag.

Trevor-Roper, H. R. (1961). *Hitler's Secret Conversations, 1941–44.* New York: New American Library.

_____ (1964). The Führer and Supreme Commander of the Armed Forces, Führer headquarters, July 16, 1940, Directive No. 16, on preparations for a landing operation against England. In *Blitzkrieg to Defeat: Hitler's War Directives, 1939–1949*. New York: Holt, Rinehart, & Winston.

Waite, R. G. L. (1977). *The Psychopathic God: Adolf Hitler*. New York: Basic Books.

_____ (1981). *Hitler in World War II: Irrationality, Conjecture, Chance, Choice, and Imagination*. Phi Alpha Theta Lecture on History, SUNY, Albany.

Department of History
University of California, Los Angeles
Los Angeles, California 90024

The Relationship of Psychosexual Development to the Successful Exercise of Power in a Woman Ruler: A Study of Catherine dé Medici

A B B Y A D A M S-S I L V A N, Ph.D., and
M A R K S I L V A N, Ph.D.

THIS STUDY OF CATHERINE DÉ MEDICI is descriptive rather than explanatory, an informed speculation regarding the dynamics and character of one whose history — not presence — is available to us. Although we lack details about Catherine's inner experience, we *do* have the scope of her entire life on which to base our ideas. From the accomplishments and failures of historical figures in their public and private lives, we can hope to identify salient strengths, deficits, flaws, and patterns (Stein, 1977).

This paper is part of a longer study of three queens — Mary, Queen of Scots, Elizabeth I, and Catherine dé Medici — who were pivotal in the political maelstrom of sixteenth-century Europe. Because these women wielded great power, their accomplishments — or the lack thereof — were glaringly reflected in the magnifying mirror of national events. They become, then, specially suita-

Abby Adams-Silvan is Associate Clinical Professor, New York University Post-Doctoral Program in Psychoanalysis and Psychotherapy; Member and Faculty, New York Freudian Society and Psychoanalytic Training Institute.
Mark Silvan is on the faculty of the New York University Post-Doctoral Program in Psychoanalysis and Psychotherapy; Member and Faculty, New York Freudian Society and Psychoanalytic Training Institute.

ble subjects for the examination of factors associated with the exercise and maintenance of power by women.

The subject that interests us is the apparent course and outcome of the feminine development of these Queens, especially as it applies in their relationship to their kingdoms as though to an apparent object. Their capacity to relate in this way, as though to an object, especially an object in which maternal impulses are invested, appear to be directly reflected in their use of power.

Our thesis is that just as there is a continuum of success for our Queens, so also is there a continuum of sexual— i.e., feminine— maturation. This continuum is in turn related to an ultimate capacity to utilize actively that femininity, most particularly in its maternal aspects, in the constructive use of power. That is, the extent to which a woman can use her mature femininity and maternal energy in the service of executive power will be an important determinant in her success. We certainly do not maintain that the line of development toward feminine maturity is the only source of successful execution of power. Skill, intellect, a variety of talents as well as masculine and bisexual identifications and a host of other characteristics inevitably come into play for a female ruler. We do, however, believe that for a woman ruler, the success or failure of feminine psychosexual development constitutes a potent variable in the success or failure with which that political power is wielded.

We do not, of course, minimize the extreme complexity of social factors influencing any political outcome, but we will here attempt only to follow our single thread in the multipatterned weave of history.

Catherine dé Medici

In December of 1560, after 26 years of obscurity, Catherine dé Medici at the age of 41 unexpectedly took upon herself the government of France as active Regent for her second son, Charles IX. Thus began a lengthy reign during the Wars of Religion in which this Italian woman dominated French politics despite great unpopularity. There were, in fact, many who might have described her as "infamous" for her complicated but central role in the St. Bartholomew's Day massacre of the Huguenots. Many enigmas surround this unpredictable woman. How did so seemingly unpromising a person, at age 41, survive so well in a dangerous era while wielding great power against strong opposition inside and outside France? An alternative question is, given her skill in political maneuvering, what accounts for the long period of obscurity preceeding 1560? Perhaps a review of what is known of her youth will provide clues to help us understand the unique personality of this woman. The principal sources of our historical data for Catherine are Heretier (1963), Mahoney (1975), Sichel (1969), and Sutherland (1973).

When Catherine dé Medici was born in Florence in 1519 the economic glory of the Medici family was literally spent. She was the last of the legitimate line, and that she was female was regarded as a disaster. Both her mother and father (to whom Machiavelli had dedicated *The Prince*) died within days of her birth. Her guardians were men, primarily her granduncle, Giulio dé Medici, who later became Pope Clement VII, and the then current Pope, Leo X, also a Medici. While she was sporadically cared for by her aunt Clarice Strozzi and her grandmother, it is probably crucial to her development and processes of identification that in the main her female caretakers were servants and her principal models were male. Her removal from Florence to Rome when she was seven months old separated her from her aunt; her grandmother died when Catherine was a year old.

She lived in Rome until she was six years old. Fragile from birth, she was several times thought to be on the brink of death. Before the age of three, she suffered three serious object losses, either by death or separation: her parents, her grandmother, and her first guardian, Clarice Strozzi.

These are years that are crucial in the development and concomitant achievement of satisfactory object relations, regulation of sadistic impulses, establishment of autonomy, and early genital awareness. From these developmental sequences follows the capacity for investment of oedipal sexual attention in a male object. It is probable that that object was, in fact, Pope Leo, with whom she had spent apparently very pleasurable time, but who died suddenly when she was three—another significant loss.

Much of the content of the conversations Catherine overheard would have been dominated by talk of political manipulation, intrigue, violence, and ambition; all valued, and all masculine prerogatives. Catherine herself, in contrast, was expected to be passive, not at all aggressive, noncompetitive, and submissive—and calculatingly marital; she was to be the consort of a powerful man, but was not to assume power herself. That is, she was to be "feminine." Phallic assertiveness would have been discouraged, and she would have known that her sex determined for her a definitely secondary role. With death, mutilation and retaliatory punishment common threats in the world she inhabited, frightening images probably led to ego and superego inhibitions of aggressive impulses and a high level of anxiousness concerning loss of body intactness. Her early illness may have provided the inner screen upon which to project her own fantasies of castration and its attendant elaborations.

At six, Catherine was returned to her own villa in Florence where she lived with her 15-year-old illegitimate cousin, Ippolyte, under the direct supervision of the man who was ruling Florence, Cardinal Passerini, a vicious tyrant dedicated to defeating the efforts of the Florentine Republicans to overthrow him.

The Florentines were violently anti-Medici, in part because of the scurrilous conduct of Catherine's own father, a fact she almost certainly knew. The move represented a violent change for Catherine: loss of stable objects, and an abrupt shift of attitude toward her by those around her, since she was now an object of overt hatred and rage. The populace reacted to her as though she were her father or granduncle, openly threatening and taunting her when she appeared in public. In addition to the violent tumult surrounding her public appearances, she was subject to sadistic and repressive measures taken by Cardinal Passerini. At an age that is developmentally characterized by a thrust toward autonomy while maintaining essentially benign positive oedipal imagos, the Florence of her youth was hardly a sanguine atmosphere for such strivings. Certainly her later political life was characterized by what seemed to be a dread of strong, affirmative action, coupled with a tendency to outbreaks of impulsive behavior.

Her cousin Ippolyte appears to have provided a partial refuge, and a male in whom she invested sexual ardor. In addition, at this time, Catherine's Aunt Clarice again became available as a positive female with whom to identify. On the other hand, her only real safety lay with Clement in Rome, and he was in constant conflict with Clarice. Catherine's affection might be drawn one way, but her survival needs pulled her toward males and unstable identifications with male power. So her early latency may have served to consolidate further the need for safety despite whatever cost in inner conflict and turmoil. Even when she was firmly in power, she is said to have been "as always, fear-ridden, dread[ing] strong action before all else" (Sichel, 1969, p. 6).

The reality of Catherine's life required self-effacement and an adaptation to obscurity, along with an exquisite awareness of her importance in the political designs of others. Contemporaries described her at this time as precociously knowledgeable about the reactions of others to her, self-effacing, submissive, reflective, and displaying unusual mental maturity. She was said to be charming, delightful, but most subdued and physically unattractive. She was patient and apparently learned early in life that the best way to escape danger was to avoid calling attention to herself. According to Sichel (p. 429) Catherine, later in life, said, "It is better to desire what one can do until one can do what one desires." The Vicompte de Turenne, reporting to Francis I on the latency-age Catherine, is quoted by Heretier (p. 24) as saying he had never seen "a person of her age more aware of the good that is done her," and that she had "great wisdom, prudence and self-control." The interplay of her need to renounce normal exuberant exhibitionism and to maintain acute attunement to the actions and intentions of others in her surroundings played a crucial role in establishing the character traits that were subsequently responsible for both her success and her failure as a ruler.

So we suggest a personality in early latency still in some feminine flux, but based on masculine identification with serious conflict around any thrust to activity, aggression, and/or sadism. There was no reliable father figure to accept and give form to that surge toward activity, as there had been none at the crucial phallic stage in early childhood. Male figures, yes; accepting of activity, no.

As political turmoil in Florence mounted, she was sent, at age eight, to the Convent of Santa Lucia. There she lived with an austere, strict order of nuns who had adopted the ideals of the reformer Savanarola. Feminine sexuality was most assuredly not an ideal to be striven for here. Catherine did adapt to the life—as she always was able to do—but she was not fond of the nuns.

After about six months she was moved to the convent of the "Murate," the "walled ones," which, although ostensibly cloistered, was actually a place of luxury, culture, and social activity. The nuns, who were from the upper classes, received visitors of both sexes. The atmosphere may even have reawakened in Catherine memories of early childhood at the papal court. Catherine was relatively happy with the "Murate," and formed a lasting attachment to the group, supporting the convent and maintaining a correspondence with the Mother Superior, with whom she had developed a strong friendship that persisted long after she left Italy for France.

Then, at age ten, this prepubertal girl was suddenly subjected to serious sexual threat. Heretier (1963) tells us that the Florentine council proposed that she be taken from the convent and placed in a brothel, so that marriage plans for her could never be consummated. She was almost certainly informed of this plan and of suggestions that for the same purpose she be given to the soldiery to be raped, or exposed naked on the city battlements. In any event, Catherine was confronted late one night by four strange men who demanded of the nuns possession of her person. Probably in a state of terror, she cut off her hair, donned a nun's habit, and repeatedly declared to her abductors that she was a nun.

She was persuaded to leave, somehow maintaining her composure. She was marched on foot across a dying Florence by the four strangers, subjected to the sight of the suffering, plague-stricken, starving, and wounded Florentines. One of her captors — a Signor Aldobrandini — was kind to her, and she never forgot his attempts to comfort her. She subsequently interceded for him and saved *his* life when the political tide had turned, a repayment of loyalty that became a lifetime characteristic.

She was escorted back to the Convent of Santa Lucia where again living under rules of rigorous asceticism, she was forced into further adaptive containment of assertivenesss, aggression, and exhibitionism. Learning that King Francis I of France had interceded for her, she began a grateful correspondence with him and developed a strong attachment to this patron of the great Leonardo da Vinci.

With the fall of the Florentine Republic, Catherine was returned to Rome, again to be watched over and used as a political pawn by Pope Clement VIII, who had covered himself with shame for his cowardice during the sack of Rome. Contemporary reports of Catherine describe her as having many of his mannerisms and being much like him in presence. We must assume, however, ambivalence in her relationship to him, and that her modeling herself after him was conflicted, for his behavior had been quite extraordinarily disloyal and shameful, and continued to be vindictive, shifty, and unpleasant, whereas she apparently took great pride in loyalty and reliability.

In Rome, aged approximately 11 to 12, Catherine was reunited with Ippolyte, and they were close companions in undisguised affection. Rumors were rife that they would marry, and that the relationship was a strongly romantic one. But is is our belief that this relationship represented Catherine's only opportunity to achieve some substitute for the very necessary but otherwise unavailable early pubertal, secret-sharing, close peer relationship for which she was so starved. We see Catherine as the type of early pubertal child for whom lack of general activity and "deadness of affect" was the counterpart of genital anesthesia (Fraiberg, 1972). As far as we know, Catherine had never had any other little girls with which to share her confidences, fears, and explorations as she developed sexually. Nevertheless, to have engaged in a quasi-peer relationship with Ippolyte placed her in an uneven triangular relationship, this time between Clement and Ippolyte; for peer, romantic, or whatever else the relationship might have been, Catherine was to marry elsewhere, and at Clement's determination.

Indeed, she did relinquish whatever Ippolyte meant to her when she was unprotestingly betrothed to Henri, the second son of Francis I. Kept in Italy for two more years till she was deemed physically mature enough for marriage, she was then taken to France, where Clement himself performed the nuptial ceremony. Although at this time some of the changes of puberty had taken place, she had not yet reached her menarche.

Her only ally in France was her father-in-law whom she charmed with her "seriousness," intellect, and companionship in such pastimes as hunting and riding. Francis I, as described by contemporaries was strikingly like Pope Leo, who had been for Catherine a warm and loving father figure, until his sudden death when she was three. The French court was literate, gay, artistic, and Catherine added to its artistic advantages, introducing ballet and other innovations. Her father-in-law was probably the only person for whom she felt a relative trust and attachment; there never was any suggestion, however, of an overt sexual liaison between them.

A bride openly unwanted by her husband, she suffered with amazing discretion and silence 26 years of public and private humiliation. Throughout their entire marriage, her husband was flagrantly attached to a woman 20 years his senior, Diane de Poitiers.

Catherine, though creative and sophisticated, was still physically unprepossessing. Worst of all, she failed to conceive during the first ten years of her marriage. Her barrenness became extremely important when her husband's older brother died in 1537, leaving her husband and his issue in direct line for the throne. She nonetheless managed to ride out court intrigues and political pressures by remaining in the background. At one point in an appeal to her father-in-law, she offered to step down as wife to the Dauphin, and to serve any princess chosen to replace her because of her infertility. She tolerated her husband's sexual infidelities with an equanimity that seems clearly more than the protocol-dictated acceptance of a royal consort.

Descriptions of her behavior suggest to us that she did not seem to have cared to any grave degree about her sexual deprivations. Most unusual was that in all her 55 years in France, she was never the object of sexual scandal. As adolescent, wife, and widow, she surrounded herself with women, and was apparently without a heterosexual object other than her husband, to whom her relationship was decidedly dutiful. For 26 years she remained in the background of court and national politics. She maintained her equilibrium through the deaths of her protector father-in-law and, eventually, of her husband. She had reigned ten years as Queen Consort, and by the time she was widowed she had borne four sons and three daughters at close intervals, after her ten barren years. Although historical descriptions differ, the impression is that she showed no strong maternal interest in her children. There are, in fact, several descriptions of her beating her daughters rather savagely in their early adolescence. She turned over much of her children's upbringing to Diane de Poitiers, who had even assisted at their birth, and by whom they were instructed. While the delegation of maternal functions to surrogates was a regular occurrence in the noble and royal houses of the day (royal children usually had their own households), the choice of a husband's mistress for such duties is unusual. In this case, however, there are available dynamically informed explanations.

First, Diane was actually old enough to be the mother of the royal couple, and may even have served that function to some extent. But even more important we may remember that clinical evidence often supports Deutsch's (1944) contention that the opportunity to experience a close, secret-sharing, mutually exploratory peer relationship in early puberty provides an important opportunity to work through bisexual tendencies. Likewise, the opportunity to engage in a healthy, constructively terminated triangle is important for the establishment of heterosexuality in later puberty. Women who, like Catherine, either miss or have engaged in distorted versions of these experiences, may tend compulsively throughout their lives to become involved in pathological triangular relationships, either in fantasy or reality in the service of gratifying unresolved negative oedipal (homosexual) wishes. Such intentional seeking of triadic relationships supports the supposition of oedipal, rather than preoedipal dominance.

Catherine seems to have had a kind of self-control about, and acceptance of, the relationship between her husband and his mistress that suggests it provided her with some form of gratification. In fact, her only reported attempt to interfere or attenuate the affair was by manipulating Henri into a liaison with another woman, one Lady Fleming, the governess for Catherine's own daughter-in-law, Mary Stuart. In other words, she sought to break one triangle by constructing another. If she were indeed attempting to fill the unmet needs of puberty in a distorted way, that compromise would help to explain the quite bewildering historical puzzle of why Catherine displayed such a startling lack of animosity toward Diane both before and after the King's death.

At the death of her husband, Henri II, Catherine's oldest son, Francois II assumed the throne. He reigned for 17 months, dying suddenly of a brain abscess, after which Catherine assumed power as regent to Charles IX, never to relinquish it during her lifetime.

The Timing of Catherine's Assuming Power

Besides many nonpsychological factors, we assume that there had to be an intrapsychic or unconscious component to Catherine's assumption of power at this time in particular, especially because only 17 months earlier her elder son, the new king Francois II had granted her "full authority as governor of France" (Heretier, 1963, p. 78). He is said to have begged her to assume control, a plea she rejected. Instead, she allowed this rather weak, albeit violent, young man and his arrogant and grandiose wife, Mary Stuart, to bring Mary's French uncles into almost total authority.

At that time, Catherine may have been fearful of her own aggression and reacted defensively by a compensatory show of passivity. The sudden violent death of her husband, Henri II, had been predicted to Catherine by Nostradomus, the court astrologer, in whom Catherine had complete confidence. She herself had had a premonitory dream before the tournament in which the King was accidentally killed. Although she had tried to keep Henri from participating in the joust, she had not been successful and held herself partially responsible for his death. Catherine's relationship to her husband Henri probably was highly ambivalent: he had rejected her flagrantly and had been openly hostile to his father, Catherine's father-protector, King Francois I.

In addition, she had particular reason to hate Mary Stuart, her daughter-in-law and the new queen, who had referred to her as a "Florentine shopkeeper," taunting her as she had been taunted so many years before, publicly humiliating Catherine, and making no effort to curb her own arrogant superiority.

All these factors may have stimulated Catherine's conflicts around sadism and dominance which had been necessarily hidden and overcontrolled throughout her psychosexual development.

Another interesting possibility is suggested by a historical fact revealed in the role book of the convent of the Murate in the Archives of Tuscany in Florence. If they are accurate, then the Mother Superior who had been in residence at the convent when Catherine was boarded there, and of special importance to her, died in 1560. This, Catherine would almost certainly have known, since they were in active correspondence and she was benefactress to the convent. Within the realm of possibility is that with the death of the Mother Superior Catherine finally put to rest a fantasy of rejoining the convent she had never wished to leave, and of a reunion with a benign mother figure. (We should point out in this context that her characteristic style of dress was much like the habit of a nun.)

Further, one may wonder if she finally mastered a complex combination of devotion, rivalry, rage at abandonment, and unresolved ambivalence toward the Mother Superior by an identification with a powerful asexual maternal figure which brought her out of her primarily passive, "humble" mode into a more active executive stance when her second opportunity for power arrived.

For 30 years Catherine ruled as the unquestioned power and policy-maker through years of excruciating turbulence; now as Regent, now as Queen Dowager. To reverse Valery's aphorism on consciousness: "It reigns but it does not govern," Catherine governed, though she did not reign; always operating behind the persona of a man as the executor of policies she advocated. Although she became an extraordinarily active executive and political manipulator, she never gave up the façade of a shadowy, neutral presence behind a male figure. To her kingdom she maintained a dark, asexual presence, even to the extent of wearing black for the duration of her reign. At best her personality was considered obscure, enigmatic; more generally she was regarded as wily, devious, without compassion, and most significantly, untrustworthy — indeed, by many, as an evil, amoral political genius.

She was hated in her lifetime and believed to be the most important instigator of flagrant and unnecessary bloodshed, such as the St. Bartholomew's Eve massacre. She died alone, neglected and reviled, in spite of her extraordinary achievements in maintaining the national and international integrity of France.

Discussion

It is our understanding of Catherine that her personality reflected the isolation, withdrawal of affect, negative self-image, and weak object cathexis of an extraordinarily intelligent but depressed woman. It seems to us that she regressed primarily to negative oedipal and phallic levels through a combination of an early deprivation of consistent maternal care and a basically masculine identification that was defensive and therefore far from optimal in nature. This was in conjunction with an atmosphere where the sexual consolidations of latency, and sexual strivings of puberty and adolescence were conflicted, so that those strivings seem to have been abandoned in favor of a passive acceptance of her sexuality as the political pawn it had always represented to the men governing her life. Her sexual self-image coincided with their image of her, and she apparently never experienced a mature, pleasurable adult sexual relationship.

Further, the need for an intense awareness and sensitivity to the moods and unspoken wishes of those around her may have led to a hypercathexis and fixation of voyeuristic impulses. An interesting quasi-clinical corroboration of this is to be found in reports that during her marriage she was reported to have had holes drilled into the floor of the apartment above that shared by Henri and Diane de Poitiers, and that, in company with several ladies-in-waiting, she observed her husband with his mistress. This is also consonant with our suggestion that Catherine was seriously affected not only by early infantile but also by pubertal psychic deprivation: she still sought the friend who would share her intimate secrets, and the intensification of the triangular experience in attempts to work through the sexual — and especially bisexual — tensions of puberty.

It is impossible to know the reason for her long-delayed menarche and subsequent years of sterility, but irrespective of the sequential interplay of cause and effect, those facts had to be associated with further damage to her feminine self-concept.

The inhibition of activity necessitated by her life circumstances made open assertion dangerous. It was adaptive, though in the long run deleterious, for Catherine had early to abandon any adjustment based on overactivity or active power modes. Rather, in life and in her political career, she utilized and manipulated others against each other to achieve her goals. Her proclivity for, and pleasure in, secret machinations, as well as her skill in maneuvering through the intrigues and kaleidoscopic changes of personal alliances, may have been partially derived from the unfulfilled feminine needs of puberty, her kingdom a ground for enacting her secretiveness and manipulations. While surely useful politically, that secretiveness was probably unnecessarily excessive, and led to the intense mistrust and dislike that characterized the attitude of her people toward her. Expediency, which would surely have been condoned in a male ruler of the sixteenth century, was reviled in her. This might have been mitigated if she could have been perceived, as was Elizabeth I of England, as a woman capable of feminine and maternal love, as well as effectively wielding the authority of state.

Since her female gender role (i.e., wife and mother) had never had consistent suitable feminine or maternal ego ideals, she was further handicapped in her capacity to develop a suitable self-concept as a woman. Repression and denial rather than sublimation appear to characterize her feminity. She was never "the mother of her people"; she was experienced as calculating and without affection for her subjects. She herself seems "always to confuse compromise and even weakness with compassion" (Heretier, p. 129). Her only observed affections were for protective "fathers" (Leo, Francois I, Montmorency, a trusted friend holding considerable power). Otherwise, men — her advisors, her sons — served as phallic executors of her policies.

We are proposing that Catherine's psychological development proceeded to the oedipal level, albeit with considerable conflict, especially around negative oedipal objects, but that her experience in latency, in conjunction with early object deprivation, made her hold on adolescent genitality shaky. By the time she was 15, she had retreated to solving, not resolving, her sexual conflicts by a repression and renunciation that characterized the remainder of her life. Additionally, it is possible that her occasional but historically crucial orchestrations of violence and her facile recoveries may represent some aspect of attempts to master the traumata around the violence of her childhood.

In general, she related to her kingdom in the detached, sometimes impulsive, often hesitant asexual and frigid manner that made her personally mistrusted and limited the constructive use of her power. She treated her people as she had been treated, without true empathy or relatedness, maintaining a shadowy presence with extraordinary political skill. To her people she was the competent but withdrawn mother, a Mother Superior. To France she was a loyal and effective but frigid spouse.

Summary and Conclusions

We have now examined some biographical data with special reference to the libidinal vicissitudes of Catherine dé Medici, one of three queens against whom John Knox railed in his "First Blast of the Trumpet Against this Monstrous Regiment of Women" sermon.

One element in the relative success or failure in the use of power by each of these queens seems to be associated with the level of psychosexual maturity on which she eventually functioned, and the concomitant manifestation of that maturity in her relationship to her kingdom as to an object.

Mary Stuart, the least effective of the three, was the most poorly developed psychosexually. Demanding constant admiration, she relied on seduction and personal charm; her femininity was characterized by exhibitionism, impulsivity and narcissism. Her maternity was characterized by neglect and what looks to have been an easy abandonment of attachment in favor of her own gratification. She seems to have sexualized her political undertakings and attempted to exercise power by utilizing infantile mechanisms, most especially her personal charm, to manipulate others. Her people — children — were narcissistic extensions of herself, her kingdom an object with which she enacted a compulsion to humiliate and be humiliated.

A study of the life of Elizabeth the Great suggests that her sexual development was the most sturdy of the three, and that she was able, through much of her life, to act in an assertively feminine way. She experienced herself as a Mother-Queen, apparently obtaining sufficient satisfaction to compensate for the deprivation of real maternal satisfaction. Her kingdom was a spouse to whom she was committed and faithful and loving. "I am already married to a husband, which is the people of England," (Jenkins, 1962, p. 370).

Her political style seems to reflect an active femininity and a capacity for sublimation. She seems to have used, but not been dominated by, a masculine identification. "Ye may have a greater prince, but ye shall never have a more loving prince," (Jenkins, 1962) she says, but she also referred frequently to her subjects as her "children" and she their "mother."

Catherine dé Medici's relationship to her kingdom reflected her problems with a feminine and maternal identification which, though minimally available till early latency, could not be consolidated into her personality because of early object deprivation in conjunction with overt sexual restriction and traumata late in the latency period. For her, instinctual renunciation was of critical importance for survival. Voyeuristic tendencies but an adaptive need to inhibit stringently her exhibitionism were salient in her character, and perhaps related to her effective, shadowy exercise of political power.

Catherine's serious limitations as a ruler may be considered to be primarily in the negative attitude toward her held by her subjects, as well as by subsequent generations. Although religious issues surely played an important role, her unpopularity as a ruler may be ascribed in part to her inability fully to develop as a loving woman and mother.

The psychosexual schema we have suggested represents an advance from Mary, Queen of Scots, but did not take her as far as Elizabeth. That relative failure in feminine and maternal maturation corresponds to her relative position on our continuum of success and failure in the maintenance and use of power.

Two conclusions are suggested by our study. First, the achieving woman need not rely primarily on the masculine component of her personality if she is to wield power successfully, rather the effective attainment of mature femininity may be an equally crucial factor. Second, the work of governing can become a quasi-object related to with the same dedication that a woman devotes to the sexual and maternal objects in her life; and the converse, a woman ruler who is impaired in her devotion to sexual and maternal objects will be limited in her capacity to exercise authority and power optimally.

REFERENCES

Deutsch, H. (1944). *The Psychology of Women, vol. I, II.* New York: Grune & Stratton, 1965.
Fraiberg, S. (1972). Genital arousal in latency girls. *Psychoanal. Study Child,* 27:439–475. New York: Int. Univ. Press.
Heretier, J. (1963). *Catherine dé Medici,* trans. C. Haldene. London: Allen & Unwin.

Jenkins, E. (1962). *Elizabeth and Leicester*. New York: Coward McCann.
Mahoney, I. (1975). *Madame Catherine*. New York: Coward McCann Geoghagan.
Sichel, E. (1969). *The Later Years of Catherine dé Medici*. London: Dawson's of Pall Mall.
Stein, M. H. (1977). A psychoanalytic view of mental health: Samuel Pepys and his diary. *Psychoanal. Q.*, 46:82–116.
Stoller, R. J. (1973). *Splitting*. New York: Quadrangle Books.
Sutherland, N. M. (1973). *Catherine dé Medici and the Ancient Regime*. London: Macmillan.

300 Central Park West
New York, N.Y. 10024

The Plight of the Imposturous Candidate: Learning Amidst the Pressures and Pulls of Power in the Institute

HELEN K. GEDIMAN, Ph.D.

PSYCHOANALYTIC INSTITUTES ARE SOMETIMES more or less "taken in" by candidates who suffer from imposturous tendencies of one degree or other. Supervisors, evaluators, Progression Committee members may constitute, for the candidate with imposturous tendencies, the "audience" that inadvertently heightens imposturous ego trends. Supervisors may unwittingly reinforce a candidate's "false self" because they are susceptible, as are we all, to identifying unconsciously with the wished-for omnipotence that the imposturous candidate expresses so obviously and ego-syntonically (see Gediman, 1985). What has been identified, often after a long-delayed recognition, as a form of pathological imposture may indeed resemble, phenomenologically, the first steps of the normal process of learning to become a psychoanalyst. In the beginning, we are not surprised if we observe a certain degree of unintegrated role-playing. In addition, the neophyte trainee is encouraged to assume, in a controlled and limited sense, multiple identifications with both patients and supervisors in order to develop empathy and analytic wisdom.

Helen K. Gediman, Ph.D., is Clinical Professor of Psychology, New York University Postdoctoral Program in Psychoanalysis and Psychotherapy; Faculty, New York Freudian Society.

We would hope that in the candidate, the multiple identifications are temporary and goal-related and not indicative of the poorly integrated identity of those suffering from serious imposturous tendencies, but unfortunately such is not always the case. It is particularly not the case when a candidate who *does* suffer from imposturous tendencies comes up against the real power of the institute. The power issue comes into all "tilted" relationships (Greenacre, 1954). And in supervision, we have two tilted relationships, tilted by virtue of the real power invested in the supervisor by both the candidate and the institute. Imposture, in those with significant imposturous tendencies, may be one pathological way of adapting to a real power structure when one's own survival in the institute is dependent on identification with the values, expectations, and roles of the "powers that be." In what follows I attempt to illustrate, at some length, how the distortions of the tilted reality made by an imposturous supervisee often take the form of shifting, mimicking, poorly integrated identifications.

Because a certain degree of role-playing in our candidates is expectable, and functions to serve adaptively to real power, we often miss noticing that it might also suggest a learning or characterological difficulty. When, for example, it persists too long, we should then suspect that we may be dealing with a form of imposture. Such imposturous candidates are often discovered, eventually, and often too belatedly, by supervisors who finally recognize that they have been "hoodwinked." When the supervisors report the difficulty, the candidate may be labeled character-disordered even "psychopathic," and dropped from the institute. Why does it often take so long to recognize such trainees, other than the reasons just offered regarding stages in the learning process? I suggest that perhaps we are too easily "conned" by our "clones." My use of slang is intended to emphasize the importance of the major idea it expresses: we embrace our ideal selves when we think we see them in our students, whose ideal is to be like us by "acting" like us.

And further, I would emphasize that in the ascending triadic systems (patient → analyst → supervisor), (analyst → supervisor → institution) involved in the supervisory situation, there is always the important issue of real power. In the "real" world (Freud's "material" reality) as opposed to the intrapsychic world (psychic reality) there is real power.

Real power *presses* on any candidate insofar as the supervisor evaluates his or her progress, or will have a say about eventual graduation, or even about referrals, promotions, and degree of success as an eventual peer. Howard Shevrin (in Wallerstein, 1981) explains how his "coolness" and exaggerated "objectivity" were open to criticism as modes of analyzing by the supervision study group. According to Shevrin, these modes were due in part to his conviction that the institute expected a cool, objective approach from him, and that his evaluation at the institute and his full-time job depended on it. It was thus only natural for him to emulate his supervisor. Shevrin is quick to point out how these factors of emulation and identification (which are typical of the imposturous) do not relate exclusively to resistance and intrapsychic conflict, but also to institutional role conflict and the theoretical commitments embodied as institutional policy. He goes so far as to conclude that the supervisor-teacher should not have real administrative power and believes that it is unresolved institutional role conflict, based on real social forces, that continues to alienate and infantilize some supervisees.

In my review of Wallerstein's book (Gediman, 1984), I noted how real institutional role conflict (material reality) may be drawn into the orbit of intrapsychic conflict and the transferences and countertransferences (psychic reality) of all three participants in triadic systems:

This possibility would not preclude that institutionally related role conflicts may not have been operating autonomously (i.e., in and of themselves), relatively unrelated to significant unresolved intrapsychic conflict issues of any of the parties involved. One might then have hard evidence that a decision to be secretive [or imitative] in order to be politically wise may be more or less neurotically motivated at the same time as it is an adaptive decision simply to be politically wise [p. 423].

Because learning to be an analyst and learning to be an analysand lend themselves readily both to *feeling* imposturous and, in some instances, to being imposturous in troublesome ways, it is important to evaluate imposturous tendencies in the context of imitation on the way toward internalization as a normal developmental phase of childhood and of imitation as a normal phase in the learning process on the way toward integrated identifications with analysts.

When the way candidates report to the supervisor seems to be only simply mimicry, reminiscent of childlike role-modeling and patterning of prescribed technique; and when they undergo kaleidoscopic shifts in what is purportedly analytic behavior; and when, in reporting, they enact unreflectively what they believe to be their patient's personality, we do well to suspect character tendencies toward the "as-if" imposturous, above and beyond a normal learning phase. The candidates delude themselves, as it were, with their own impersonations of an idealized imago of the "the analyst." It is particularly the unreflective, imitative enactments, often in an attempt to adapt to perceived real power, that constitute the "pathological parallelisms" par excellence of imposture, phenomena that I include in my illustrative case of Dr. E.

Since imitation or role-playing would normally be a precursor of more consolidated identifications in learning to do analysis, it is only over time and, at that, often very difficult that we can draw the line between what is normal and phase-specific imitative learning, on the one hand, and the role-playing and imitativeness of pathological imposture, on the other. To aid in drawing that fine line, it will be necessary to show that the disturbances in the sense of reality of the imposturous individual are extreme variations of some important but specifically goal-directed requirements of doing and learning to do analysis. For example, trainees *must* make trial and flexible identifications. This requirement is more "dangerous" for some than for others, particularly for those whose fundamental reality sense is disturbed precisely by virtue of multiple, shifting identifications, the very process required in conducting analysis. A therapist *must* empathize with the patient, but if one's point of contact is exclusively either the patient's primitive unconscious, or more superficial peripheral aspects that may be imitated, important failures in empathy will ensue. The very fineness of this line makes it difficult to discern and may delay the detection of serious imposture for a long time, even in the very best of institute settings.

An additional problem is the ubiquity of a spectrum of transitory to stabilized "as-if" states which are to be found among the normal as well as among the characterologically imposturous. Since a consolidated professional identity does not develop until late in the learning process, early detection of imposture is understandably difficult except in blatantly psychopathic cases. One might pose the question this way: Will the supervisor's conveyance or demonstration of the analytic approach, which ideally should parallel or reflect the essence and not the superficial "technology" of the analytic process, lead to deep, consolidated, flexible identifications, or will it lead only to mere shallow imitations? The imposturous candidate is indeed an extreme example of failed identification with the analyst's fundamental way of working. Although it may be rare, a contaminating influence might be discerned in imitations of the training analyst who really could be conducting the candidate's analysis with significant inauthenticity. There are, however, many in-between situations where problems result from various real faulty teaching and learning situations, the consequences of which may not be too easy to distinguish from the characterological problems of the candidate. It is here that the designations made by the COPE Study Group of "dumb spots" (difficulties due to learning problems or inexperience) and "blind spots" (characterological or countertransference difficulties) as related to one another would be well considered.

It has been said that knowledge of the gospel is not sufficient to preach well and honestly. Fred Wolkenfeld (personal communication, 1983) suggested the gospel analogy for understanding an aspect of this important relationship between imitation and reportorial honesty in the learning process. To carry through the analogy of the clergy's use of the self in the transmission of religion and spirituality to the *use of the self* in the psychoanalytic learning situation, knowledge of the "analytic gospel" alone precludes, in part because of its tilt toward the real power pulls, the essential process of doing analysis. This unique requirement of our work has been called by many names: internalizations, identifications, transformations of the self into the cohesive analytic self, or the development of the candidate's potential as an analyzing instrument. A student's attempt to present to a supervisor the gospel truth of his or her sessions with a patient, even though really encouraged by some supervisors, could be fundamentally "dishonest" — as will be seen in the illustrative case of Dr. E.

Another real situation exerting a powerful pull for imposture, and found in all institutes, relates to the candidates' being required to work with several supervisors who work differently from one another. While such differences in ways of working are to be found in even the most homogeneous of training settings, they would be particularly marked in institutes that offer training in more than one theoretical orientation and that encourage "interdisciplinary" crossing back and forth. The shifting multiple vantage points and work-ego identities required to "go with" multiple ways also require adroit, flexible shifting which could potentiate any latent, imposturous tendencies of fluidity and facileness in candidates predisposed in that direction.

Yet another otherwise very valuable, indeed essential, characteristic of the training process that is also conducive to imposture among the vunerable is to be found in rapport, engagement, and mutual give-and-take between supervisor and candidate. The supervisor's authentic positive input and feedback and validation sustains, heightens, and enhances the subjective sense of integrity and cohesiveness of all supervisees, perhaps even more so in the case of the imposturous than of the nonimposturous. Thus, the requisite positive climate may hold serious masking potential for imposture. Greenacre (1958a, 1958b) noted that the "false" self becomes reflected back, magnified, and strengthened with such mirroring affirmation. So, supervisory situations in which there is good rapport, comfort, and engagement may benefit the self-experience and learning experience of the average-expectable candidate in average-expectable ways, but could have the unfortunate effect of impeding the detection of possible imposturousness for a long time.

Greenacre's (1958b) published thoughts on the connection between the artist and the impostor have alerted us to the reverse phenomenon, that is, *feeling* and *fearing* that we are imposturous when we are not. I think it is common that analysts in training, like the artists to whom Greenacre refers, feel and fear that they are impostors, especially at the beginning of their careers. The fact that various "selves," or more exactly, variations on one "self," are required for analytic work may lead to some of the same fears. That is, the analyst and the artist make changes in self-presentation and self-organization, specific and limited to doing analysis or to creative aesthetic work, respectively. Among the imposturous, these limits do not hold.

Illustrative Case Material[1]

For reasons of accessibility and confidentiality, I am limiting my case illustration to a trainee in psychoanalytic psychotherapy who was not and never has, to my knowledge, become a candidate at a psychoanalytic institute. I subscribe to the idea that there are continuities between the process of psychoanalytic therapy and that of psychoanalysis proper, as well as their supervisees, and so my data should suffice.

The illustrative material will place particular emphasis on the aforementioned disturbances in the sense of reality and how these disturbances differ from average-expectable, phase-acceptable learning processes. I have prepared one reasonably lengthy illustration, Dr. E., to exemplify the problem of hypertrophied and limited empathy and other disturbances in the sense of reality. The material will also include a consideration of imposture as typifying, par excellence, a pathological parallelism: i.e., where problems with multiple, shifting identifications leading to a deficient understanding of the treatment process as reflected in work with the patient is repeated or enacted in parallel fashion in supervision. Such a pathological parallelism, when found in a trainee with the vulnerabilities

---

[1]The data presented here are not psychoanalytic. That is, they derive from process notes of a supervisory and not a psychoanalytic or psychotherapeutic relationship. Therefore, my references regarding pathology, including those implying fragmented identifications and difficulty in distinguishing self from object and object from object, may not be as reliable as those deriving from the psychoanalytic situation. They should nonetheless serve.

under scrutiny here must, I believe, be regarded in part as a result of the experience of powerlessness and fragility which an individual with imposturous tendencies would inevitably feel in a training institute.

This kind of enactment is but one form of parallel process, defined (Gediman & Wolkenfeld, 1980; Wolkenfeld, 1984) as a multidirectional representational system in which major psychic events, including complex behavioral patterns, affects, and conflicts, occurring in one dyadic situation — analysis or supervision — are repeated in the other. A nonpathological parallelism, then, could also reflect multiple, shifting identifications, but where they are nonproblematic and remain within the limits of the requirements of doing analytic work. In keeping with my main thesis, then, issues of powerlessness and fragility would not emerge as importantly in these "average-expectable" parallelisms as they do in the pathological parallelisms found among trainees, like Dr. E., who suffer from significant imposturous tendencies.

Supervisee E.

Although my case material focuses manifestly on illustrating problems with imposture, it would be well to keep in mind, throughout, the corollary issue of power-impact, which is always suggested and always a significant though sometimes latent motivating force underlying Dr. E.'s difficulties in supervision. The supervisor is, after all, not simply a teacher, but an evaluator and a critically determining influence on the student's future, as well. Dr. E. is not representative of the more average-expectable degrees of imposture, but stands as a conglomerate of fairly extreme imposturous tendencies. This tilted weighting should be heuristically valuable for comparison with the average-expectable degree of "as-if-ness" which is inherent in the early stages of the psychoanalytic learning process.

Dr. E. illustrates hypertrophied "empathy-like" responses (see Khron, 1974) in the trainee in psychoanalytic psychotherapy, as well as prototypically imposturous trends related to difficulties in establishing a center of gravity or orientation. Dr. E. was notable as a supervisee compliant to the letter with all that her supervisor asked of her, but she had great difficulty in grasping the spirit of the enterprise. She had originally taken verbatim notes and read them during supervisory sessions. The resulting material had a lifeless, distant, isolated quality. As a corrective and in an attempt to get her to loosen up, I suggested she take minimal process notes in the hope that she could then focus more on engaging with me as supervisor. She followed that suggestion by producing masses of noncohesive material that she "extemporaneously" reported. When I was troubled enough to comment to her about the inauthentic sound of the material presented this way, she revealed that she had still taken six or seven pages of verbatim notes, as lengthy as ever, but since I did not want her to read them in the sessions, she had read them over assiduously in advance of our supervisory session and had been conscientiously repeating them from memory. She revealed this with no apparent insight into the absurdity of her actions. By committing her verbatim notes to memory and then reporting what she remembered, she was acting "as if" she were spontaneous, while in fact she was more stimulus-bound than ever. Whatever characterological problems contributed to this style, an intense anxiety to placate the "powers that be" was also operative.

Yet, despite this "blind" and/or "dumb" spot, she seemed to catch on extraordinarily quickly to the drift of my questions and hunches concerning the patient, and she confirmed all too readily any psychodynamic hunches that she discerned lay behind my questions. She never, however, spontaneously introduced any hunches of her own. The problem that aroused my suspicions was that she started to report as verbatim material something that immediately confirmed my speculative hypothesis, as though it had naturally followed at just that point in the memorized notes of the session at which I had intervened. She appeared to finish my very sentences as soon as I introduced the thought that started them. She acquired a center of gravity, with its excessive attention to the expectations of others, and thus an excess of misdirected and superficial "empathy," toward what she thought I was asking for. It was as though I represented a doctrine to which she must adhere, unselectively, in order to fulfill her requirement.

I should like to expand here on the shifty way this prototypically imposturous supervisee had of reporting allegedly verbatim material, reminiscent of certain "borderline" or hysterical patients who lapse into "pseudologia fantastica" when they become involved in conveying their experience to another. Dr. E. repeatedly "replayed" vividly a conversation that had taken place between her patient, a man, and a friend of his. It was though she had been where that conversation had taken place and never in the place—her consulting room—where the patient had reported the conversation to her. That is, she and the interaction between herself and her own patient, and her emotional-cognitive responses to him, were simply not present in the material she reported to me. Her point of orientation, or center of gravity, seemed now to be located too "empathically" where the original extra-analytic event took place. She reproduced the latter with such uncannily sounding "accuracy" that I began to suspect it could not be entirely true except in her imagination.

When such a supervisee enacts what a patient was saying about a friend or gives an apparently nearly verbatim account of what a friend told a patient, or what a patient told a friend, *but from the friend's point of view,* there is too much positioning "inside the friend's head." This positioning leaves out entirely what might have been happening in the therapy or analytic session itself with respect to the way the patient was talking, associating, relating, and the way the supervisee as analytic therapist was listening and engaged in interaction with the patient.

Such a supervisee surely appears to be behaving in a psychopathic manner, but is this really so? Like all supervisees, Dr. E. was under real pressure to produce what was expected of her in order to fulfill her training requirements. But unlike all, she might be described as "shifty," not in the more psychopathic sense of being evasive or of producing "fudged" and phony psychotherapeutic data, but as related to nonsolidity and nonrootedness with respect to intrapsychic and interpersonal centers of gravity and boundaries. The way she conveyed no contact with what transpired between her patient and herself was consistent with the manner that her contact with me appeared limited to reading or presenting verbatim notes from memory. When I called the problem to her attention, she said that she was doing the kind of "experiential reporting" she had been taught by former supervisors. Here, too, it sounded to me as though she were imitating what she thought experiential reporting should be without at all understanding its spirit or purpose in the teaching and learning of psychotherapy. The plaguing problem was at least twofold: *whose* experience was being reported and *what kind* of notes were these where the patient's extra-analytic interactions with significant others were reported with such suspiciously vivid detail?

To check out my hunch, which had become a conviction, that I was dealing with an "as-if" trainee with significant imposturous tendencies, I decided on a new teaching strategy of withholding "mirroring" and feedback. Since the more pathological hypertrophied "empathic" attunement is highly selective in areas relevant to narcissistic gratifications, the fluency of its expression is prone to slippage into arbitrary fluidity once the "other" does not offer enough cues as to how well the supervisee is doing or as to what is "expected." And what is expected may have real consequences for survival in the institute, reinforcing preexisting imposturous tendencies. If supervisory mirroring, or the gleam in the supervisor's eye, is withheld, if the supervisor is "laid back," opaque, refraining from engaging in mutual but potentially "cuing-in" exchanges, the imposturous supervisee may lapse from "as-if" reporting of sessions into communications, the meaning of which are difficult to track; the supervisee could even lapse into extremely disjointed and confused reporting. I decided to remain, to a degree exceedingly greater than would be found in my characteristic supervisory style, more silent, "laid back," nonengaging, opaque, passive.

When I actually remained silent for an entire session, I could hardly make head or tail or the material Dr. E. was reporting. There was nothing that I could empathize with as authentic, that is, as something that one would reasonably expect to transpire between an analytic therapist and patient. Little held together cohesively, consistently, or systematically in the manner of any psychoanalytic reporting or process with which I was familiar, or which would be recognized as such, consensually, by other analysts. It became apparent that her role-playing at what she believed was expected of her became all the more hollow, false, inauthentic, when I no longer provided the scaffolding, structure, schemata, when I was no longer the colluding audience. When I confronted my supervisee with this difficulty, I sensed bewilderment, stress, a slight degree of muted anger, perhaps. Now there was "trouble in paradise," in contrast to the previous apparent harmony, which looked retrospectively like "sham" interaction and sham engaging rapport. At most, she could sound like a child imitating what she thought she should sound like in the role of an adult analyst delivering an "objective" interpretation. Here is a prime example of the sense of powerlessness among the nontalented — imposturous or otherwise.

But don't we expect role-playing and imitation in the early stages of psychoanalytic education for most of our trainees, including the very talented? It is only when this imitative phase persists long beyond the beginning that we may be dealing with serious pathology and not simply with a normal phase in the learning process. After all, it was not until well into our work that I realized that role-playing seemed to be mostly all that Dr. E. could do. She was not progressing toward a consolidated identity as an analytic therapist, and, unconsciously, she must have sensed her inner powerlessness to do so. Nonetheless, I persisted, without yet realizing that my very persistence was an exercise of real power which only increased her bewilderment and deep anxieties.

Other interesting things began to happen with Dr. E. once I decided, as a "corrective," to be more opaque, and once I had confronted her with her problem in locating a center of gravity in her experiential reporting. We no longer, of course, engaged in the pseudomutuality and "give-and-take" that had felt so rewarding to me for approximately a year. I ceased mirroring her responses, which were informed by a vast but superficial and eclectic knowledge of many points of view to which she had been exposed but where her breadth of knowledge surely exceeded her depth of grasp. As I began to be convinced of the lack of depth in her grasp of the knowledge she was vainly trying to assimilate, I also had an increasingly difficult time in "getting a reading" on her patient. This difficulty was due not only to my increased awareness of her difficulties and my consequent reserve at inadvertently "cuing" her in, but also to her increasingly evident lapses into fragmented, disconnected, now more obviously "inauthentic" reporting. I confronted her with this difficulty, suggesting once again that she stop trying to take or to memorize any detailed process notes, but to come in simply with an outline that she could fill in from memory. I also explicitly told her that I would just listen for a while for I was concerned that our interactions themselves were biasing her mode of reporting.

She then came with no notes at all. She made obvious gestures at searching diligently in the back of her memory for what had happened in the sessions. She engaged in "as-if" reporting, which, without my "cues," sounded to me very incoherent and unfollowable, confirming my hunch about the conditions under which hypertrophied but selective empathy-like responsiveness *fails*. She, too, noticed her increasing incoherence and actually proposed that she was having difficulties in empathizing and therefore in reporting accurately to me because her *patient* was a slippery "as-if" personality and that was a very difficult thing for her to convey accurately in supervisory sessions!

Now, was this student an *impostor*? She did not literally pretend under cover of someone else's name. But she did something very much like that. She pretended under cover of someone else's style and role. She was masquerading herself, psychologically speaking, in the name of a version of psychoanalytic psychotherapist which was not well internalized, but which corresponded to her reading of the expectations and pressures of the training institution.

The question now facing us is, how was this masquerader similar to and how did she differ from *any* student in the beginning phases of learning, phases which should lead to the optimal use of oneself as an analyzing instrument. Even if we accept Deutsch's (1955) view that imposturous tendencies may be found in all human beings, and that the average expectable manifestly differs only in degree from the pathologically imposturous, it is still essential to capture the very nature, the quality of that difference, in order to distinguish the seriously pathological from the psychopathology of everyday life.

First, Dr. E.'s mode of reporting was atypical. Her manner of trying to convey experiential data could be regarded as imposturous, in the artifice of both her straining for phenomenological accuracy and the obvious inauthenticity in her way of producing memorized "process notes." She was also imposturous in her technique. She fancied herself as "making interpretations" whenever she made a verbal statement of any kind to her patient. Asked why she had called a particular intervention an interpretation, she became imposturous at theorizing: "It was an interpretation because it dealt with the unconscious." Now, none of this may look like a gross deviation, for we might expect such loose approximations from any beginner, particularly a very anxious one. But in context she was glib enough to strongly suggest imposture. She knew just enough about experiential reporting; she knew just enough about psychoanalytic theories. The "give-away" was that she knew just enough about *many* theories, some of which were intrinsically incompatible with or contradictory to each other, but whose potentially vexing ambiguities did not seem to raise any question for her as they would for most thoughtful students. She could shift easily from one to another frame of reference, embracing all, and was suspiciously untroubled by theoretical incompatibilities. This propensity for an easy eclecticism embodied more anarchy than flexibility, and it suggested a "miscarrying" of the requisite personal flexibility and multiple viewpoints essential for doing analytic work. She knew just enough about technique, but it did not seem to matter to her if she functioned correctly or incorrectly. And she showed none of the expectable anxiety of a beginner making mistakes. She thought she was doing what she was supposed to do.

Dr. E., then, is not like our more usual nonimposturous beginners for whom distinctions matter and who learn about them either receptively or by actively questioning what they are doing and why, who challenge the supervisor, who don't catch on right away, and who call *themselves* into question. The better integrated neophytes are not so fearful to question, within acceptable limits, the power of authority, and do so by using their own powers of intelligence and discrimination. Rather, Dr. E. unquestioningly accepted everything as though to get on and over with a charade required for completion of training requirements. The pervasiveness of her shiftiness, the blatantly "false" quality of her presentation once I abandoned my encouraging stance in favor of a truly opaque one, revealed a fundamental imposturousness with disturbances in the sense of reality of the self and the world.

I take the liberty at this point of interrupting my case illustration to elaborate two issues. I turn here to the first, that of "what really happened in the analytic hour," which will be subsumed under the topic of "daydreams in common." Although, as I said earlier, my case illustration comes from the supervision of psychoanalytic psychotherapy and not psychoanalysis proper, I am here substituting the terms, analyst, analytic candidate, and analysand, for I believe my conclusions from the case material can be generalized to the supervision of the analytic situation proper.

Daydreams in Common

"What really happened in the analytic hour" must be reconstructed from more or less ambiguous reports from the analyst or the analyst-in-training (we are talking of the supervisory situation now). The nature of psychic reality and of "material reality" of "objective truth value" and, in particular, of how knowable one person's psychic reality is to another person are central to the problem of imposture. These issues are also central to all teaching and learning of psychoanalysis, but the particular character problems of Dr. E. illustrate the importance of psychic reality in a unique way. The supervisor never really knows what actually transpired, but has "daydreams in common" (Freud, 1907; Arlow, 1969a, b) with the patient and the therapist in a way that holds together according to certain more or less specifiable criteria. Sometimes we can only imagine or fantasize what happens. The built-in aesthetic ambiguity of our work situation lends itself so easily to crossing the line between the imaginative and empathic and the fantastic, and—this is an emphasis I believe to be new—crossing the line into the imposturous. Here we are touching on *psychic reality* which is recognizable and apprehendable, provided that the one who is attempting to convey it has access to it, as the imposturous reporter does not. Dr. E., instead, focused on a particular version of "objective reality" to cover her lack of comprehension of the other, or psychic, reality. However, Dr. E.'s efforts at presenting a so-called phenomenological reality did not even meet the criteria of "material reality" or "objective truth value." That is, her various accounts of her patient's sessions were inconsistent, discontinuous, and oversimplified representations of other people which she could not piece into analytically meaningful patterns. Not only did Dr. E.'s reports not hang together in a psychoanalytically meaningful way; they defied conventional common sense and conventions of coherence. And most important, there was little evidence for their correspondence to anything recognizable that one usually expects to be going on in the analytic situation, mainly because Dr. E.'s process reporting did not contain any graspable account of that situation.

We would expect to detect the presence of material which one expects to hear if an analysis is indeed being conducted, assuming a reasonably well-selected patient: evidence of infantile sexuality and aggression; indications of recognizable defense measures; manifestations of anxiety, shame, guilt, depression; symbolic and other representations of significant body zones and modes; accounts of self-feeling and self-esteem; accounts of separateness and oneness, and a number of other themes. If we never hear these motifs in a sustained, coherent way in the candidate's report, we may safely assume that he or she has not grasped them or picked them up and helped the patient to develop them. And if the candidate still presents process notes as though he or she were unquestionably doing analysis, we must question the authenticity of the work, just as we do when criteria of "objective truth value" are not met. What Dr. E. was doing authentically was the very best that she could, but in a fundamentally powerless way, to conform to what she believed the formally institutionalized power structure expected of her.

I resume the case of Dr. E. by way of a second digression, this time on the relevance of daydreams in common to certain *"pathological parallelism"* found among the imposturous.

Pathological Parallelisms in Imposture

One of the reasons that even a mild degree of imposture in reporting yields pathological parallelisms par excellence is that the requirements of doing analysis and the criteria for imposture, despite their significant and critical *differences,* overlap sufficiently as to encourage the phenomenon to emerge. This follows the line of thinking adopted by Gediman and Wolkenfeld (1980), according to which the structural and dynamic similarities between psychoanalysis (or psychoanalytic psychotherapy) and supervision guarantee the emergence of parallelisms in the supervisory or learning situation. Those similarities, which I now see as relevant to the issue of imposture, center on the requirement of multiple empathic identificatory processes and on the use of the self as an "analyzing instrument."

The disturbances in the sense of reality of the self which are the hallmark signs of imposture all involve some changes in self-organization and self-presentation. And so does being an analyst involve such changes. However, a most important qualification should be underscored in articulating the differences between imposture and learning to be an analyst: The analyst makes changes in self-organization and self-presentation *specific* to the immediate problems of the work and of the analytic situation. The changes in self-organization made by the imposturous supervisee and which lead to the pathological parallelisms are general and not subject to consciously deliberate choice and situational requirements. That empathy, multiple shifting identifications, and multiple "selves" are required for both analytic work and for imposture does not mean that the important differences should be ignored, for they are central to an understanding and possible remediation of the pathological parallelism.

I now return to Dr. E. to show how a pathological parallel process emerged and was handled. I left off my presentation with the significant development when Dr. E. had begun to describe her *patient* in the very terms I would have used to describe *her*, a process I would label a "pathological parallelism." She told me how her patient was one of those very slippery people whose identifications were so shallow and fluid that it was very difficult for her to grasp his experience and report it to me. She explained to me that *his* identifications were very unintegrated, and he must be an "as-if" personality. She confessed that when she was relatively quiet, she had trouble following the drift of what he was saying. Now, for the first time, she began to report about problematic interactions between her and her patient, following my addressing similar problems in the supervisory interaction. She thought the patient's slipperiness must account for *my* expressed difficulty in following the drift of her material when I decided to just listen and not cue her in. All told, she acted like someone powerlessly cornered and flailing at making use of poorly understood notions that I, in her view, was imposing on her. That was her way of surviving. But I did not see that aspect of her difficulties at the time of my work with her, for the issue of imposture was then more manifestly palpable for me than that of power.

Another interesting thing occurred around the time that I was checking out my hunches by refraining from cuing in my supervisee to what I was thinking. Dr. E. reported that her patient had begun to scrutinize her face and her voice for signs of the "correctness" of his own interpretations of his dreams and other material, and for the moral correctness, of certain of his behaviors that he was reporting. She believed that her patient saw her as fluidly shifting her views of him, and that is why, she said, he needed to scrutinize her so carefully. He then, she asserted, began to comply with one after the other of these shifting projected identifications, which he attributed as coming from her.

In this uncanny parallelism, Dr. E.'s description of her patient was suspiciously close to how I perceived her with me. Most important, this reported view of her patient's dynamics *followed* my attempt to convey to her how she was intent on demonstrating to me her version of varied and ever-changing theoretical and technical virtuosity because she expected that I wished to see her do that. The problem was that her attempts to comply resulted in the looseness and fluidity that I have already described. No doubt we both wished to understand: I her work and she her patient. The parallel pressure to know, required for daydreams in common to yield a meaningful discourse in a supervisory context, can also yield the pathological or "derailed" parallelism of the instance described. I say derailed because the supervisee presented her patient as I saw her, the supervisee, but without consciously realizing that she was doing that. It was as though she understood much, unconsciously, but could not, for reasons relevant to the fragmented identity problems of the imposturous, regard herself as the object of what she understood — projecting, instead, onto her patient. The pathological parallelism just described reflects a "projective identification": the supervisee describes the patient in terms that actually describe herself. Such a parallelism constitutes an extreme and particular example of parallel process as defined earlier — the repetition in one dyadic situation, psychotherapy or supervision, of psychic events occurring in the other. It was in observing this parallelism involving projective identification that it occurred to me that the *fluidity of perspective and the multiple viewpoints required in doing analysis and in learning to do it* might provide the situational "pull" for the emergence of the supervisee's "as-if" behavior, shared by or at least projected onto her patient as well.

In a later supervisory session — and this is to illustrate a different but somewhat related point regarding parallelisms — I shared with Dr. E. a speculative hunch that her patient favored the circumventions of ordinary obstacles to his goals and gratifications, and that this proclivity was reflected in his continual use of the "side entrance" metaphor in dreams and fantasies. I conjectured that this metaphor reflected his concerns with his multiple "successful" oedipal circumventions. The patient, for example, was having an affair with his supervisor, a married, somewhat older woman, in his on-the-job training placement. He also believed that when his psychotherapy was terminated he would be able to have a love affair with the therapist. In our next supervisory session, Dr. E. rather glibly reported to me that her patient *told her* how he notices that he uses "side entrance" metaphors to express how he circumvents ordinary obstacles. He said this metaphor reflected how he believed he could have possessed his mother and now believed he could possess the therapist. I asked Dr. E. how she thought her patient's understanding of this dynamic formulation evolved in the treatment situation. I carefully avoided any reference to the fact that the patient's apparent discovery was couched in the very terms that I myself had explicitly offered speculatively in our previous supervisory session. Dr. E. became flustered and, as usual, seemed unable to provide any pertinent sequential data. Then, as though she had empathically caught on to what was on my mind, she reversed what she had presented in her initial version and implied that *she* had interpreted it to *him* in a previous session but she forgot which one, and she had neglected to report that fact to me. You see once more how difficult it was to ascertain this supervisee's center of gravity or whose experience she was reporting. She seemed utterly confused herself and showed no sign of recollecting any actual event in which either she or her patient had "interpreted" what was *my* speculative hunch.

In a much later session, Dr. E. said she found her patient engaged in a "psychological lie." While there may be many reasons for her reporting this, in context it appears as yet another pathological parallelism. Although I have never shared with her my hunches about her artifice in reporting, her account was in keeping with her characteristic empathic-like sensitivity in selected areas, and suggested that she may have divined my suspicions, unconsciously. Specifically, the lie, or actually distortion, to which she referred had to do with her patient's reporting to her that upon completing one phase of his on-the-job training, his supervisor had seduced him sexually, when it seemed in fact to Dr. E. that it was the other way around.

She then went on to describe her patient as having borderline boundary problems. She also wondered how it was possible for a patient with such serious pathology to get A-ratings for job performance and even be offered promotions, and concluded that it must have been due to a joking connection the patient himself had made previously with what he called his many A's for "ambition and adulterous achievement." Dr. E. felt certain that anyone who prevaricated so much must have job-training problems as well.

Here was more evidence of the pathological parallelism. Something I had noted in Dr. E. as a serious characterological problem area and of which she was apparently unaware in herself (a "blind spot") and which also *constituted a learning problem for her* (a "dumb spot") emerged in her report as a parallel difficulty in her patient, the implications of which she only partially understood.

It is precisely this sort of parallelism which constitutes the prototypical example of the kind of parallel impasse requiring a certain kind of supervisory intervention. It is what Gediman and Wolkenfeld (1980) have referred to as the "by-pass." In our recent personal communications, Wolkenfeld (1984) and I have formulated the by-pass as that supervisory intervention whereby the supervisor addresses the problem indirectly, in a way analogous to an analyst offering a "deflected transference" interpretation: it is discussed as a problem for the patient as it is manifest only in extra-analytic situations and not in the here-and-now analytic interaction. The supervisory by-pass, then, avoids the here-and-now supervisory interaction and focuses only on parallel dynamic problems for the patient alone, in the hope of mitigating some "real power" influences.

Yet the emergence of such a parallelism can be read as a sign that the supervisee may know unconsciously that he or she shared the patient's problem and would like the benefit of the supervisor's wisdom. Tact, too, would dictate that remarks regarding, in this instance, imposture, boundary confusion, and identity disturbance be addressed toward the extrasupervisory sphere or to the patient's obvious difficulties. When less obvious or delicate than this supervisee's proclivity toward introjection and projection, or when *more* is really at stake, such as a candidate's suitability to be an analyst, the parallelism phenomenon could be discussed more explicitly. In the case of Dr. E., it was sufficient, at first, to indicate that her difficulties in dealing with patients' problems in this area might be something she would want to discuss in her personal analysis.

With these principles in mind, I questioned whether her patient truly had engaged in a "lie," suggesting instead that he was genuinely confused as to whether he had been led on by a woman in a position of authority, real power, if you will, or whether he himself was the more seductive one. I suggested that such confusion probably emerged in the transference as well, taking the form of his having a conviction that his therapist was encouraging him to believe in the possibility of a consummated love affair once he was "graduated" upon termination. With respect to her bewilderment about his getting A's and being accepted for advanced career training, I dealt with this additional parallelism also by by-passing any explicit reference to the supervisee's similar concerns (or concerns I imagined she might be having) about my evaluating her work so that she could advance professionally, limiting my remarks to my understanding of the patient only. I reminded her that her patient was working in a very rarefied, esoteric area of specialization, where such boundary slippage not only could go undetected but could be encouraged and rewarded. It was also clear to me from many things she had said that the patient was quite tuned in to issues of innocence and corruptibility in others and that he exercised considerable charm with people for whom these were problems. I assumed that, at least unconsciously, she "heard" my references as being relevant to herself as well.

In our final supervision sessions, a parallelism emerged which I handled not by a "by-pass," or by addressing its significance for the patient alone, but by discussing it directly and explicitly as a parallelism with the supervisee. *Lest we forget the supervisor's very real contribution to parallel process,* it should be noted that at that time I was also mulling over whether *my* "by-pass technique" to circumvent ordinary supervisory obstacles paralleled the patient's "side entrance" metaphor to circumvent oedipal obstacles. The patient had been talking about working for the coming year in a city far enough

away to preclude his continuing treatment with Dr. E., for pragmatic reasons having to do with somewhat reduced finances and the
commonplace occurrence in his field of frequent geographical
relocations. This Dr. E. learned of "*suddenly*," although I had
sensed it coming ever since she casually remarked that she had begun to discuss these peripatetic aspects of his work situation. At
that time I had asked Dr.E. when she intended to confront her patient with the obvious incompatibility between continuing analytic
therapy with her and pursuing his career elsewhere, as well as his
wishfully based belief that such a course of action would at last
make possible a love affair between himself and his therapist.

It became evident that Dr. E. never made or even considered
making such a confrontation. In fact, the patient strove to maintain
his illusion of a romance throughout the treatment and never bene-
fited from any proper therapeutic attempts to analyze that fantasy
and illusion within the transference. That Dr. E. was concerned, at
least unconsciously, that she might have seduced me into believing
she could do analysis eventually and have a collegial peer relationship with me is a highly significant related parallelism. It is also
noteworthy that she had decided to terminate supervision for pragmatic reasons: her work evaluations were open to question; she was
moving to a geographically less accessible area; and she had embarked upon certain costly life changes, all of which curtailed her
pursuit of psychotherapy training. So, I identified that parallelism
directly and as a parallelism. I pointed out that it seemed of great
significance that she, in a manner paralleling her patient's vague-
ness about terminating treatment, had drifted into a course of action involving likely termination of formal training, supervision,
and her personal analysis, and for pragmatic reasons, just like her
patient, and at an inopportune time, for she could surely benefit
from much more explicit discussion in supervision and other
spheres of her training before deciding whether or not she could call
herself an analytic therapist. (She was planning to practice
privately.)

It was indeed unfortunate that Dr. E.'s own motivations and possible wishes to repudiate them had apparently interfered with the

way she conducted the therapy, and they prevented her from dealing with her patient's critical negative transference resistance. I believe that my approach conveyed the fact that I was not seduced by *her* "psychological lie" that she was doing analytic therapy, but I do not know to what extent she registered and assimilated what I had conveyed. I also do not know if there would have been a different outcome had I handled the intitial parallelism — her describing her patient as an "as-if" personality caught in a psychological lie — directly and not via the "by-pass operation." Had I talked of the parallelism of the patient's "A" for ambitious but imposturous success in his field, and Dr. E.'s fantasied "A" for analytic therapy, I might have been decidedly correct as to a dynamic interpretation but incorrect with respect to supervisory dosage, timing, and tact. Imposture, like the teaching and learning of psychoanalysis and psychoanalytic psychotherapy, indeed poses difficult problems for therapist or analyst and supervisor alike, particularly in the light of the real power that the supervisor has to influence the future course of the supervisee's life as an analyst or analytic psychotherapist.

REFERENCES

Arlow, J. (1969a). Unconscious fantasy and disturbances of conscious experience. *Psychoanal. Q.*, 38:1–27.
———— (1969b). Fantasy, memory, and reality testing. *Psychoanal. Q.*, 38:28–51.
Deutsch, H. (1955). The impostor: Contribution to ego psychology of a type of psychopath. In *Neuroses and Character Types.* New York: Int. Univ. Press, 1965, pp. 319–338.
Freud, S. (1907). Creative writers, and daydreaming. *S.E.*, 9.
Gediman, H. K. (1984). Review of *Becoming a Psychoanalyst,* ed. R. S. Wallerstein. In *Review of Psychoanalytic Books,* 2:415–428.
———— (1985). Imposture, inauthenticity, and feeling fraudulent. *J. Amer. Psychoanal. Assn.,* 33:911–935.
———— & Wolkenfeld, F. (1980). The parallelism phenomenon in psychoanalysis and supervision: Its reconsideration as a triadic system. *Psychoanal. Q.*, 49:234–255.
Greenacre, P. (1954). The role of transference: Practical considerations in relation to psychoanalytic therapy. In *Emotional Growth.* Int. Univ. Press, 1971, pp. 627–640.
———— (1958a). The impostor. In *Emotional Growth.* New York: Int. Univ. Press, 1971, pp. 93–112.
———— (1958b). The relation of the impostor to the artist. In *Emotional Growth.* New York: Int. Univ. Press, 1971, pp. 533–554.
Khron, A. (1974). Borderline "empathy" and differentiation of object representations: A contribution to the psychology of object relations. *Int. J. Psychoanal. Psychother.,* 3:142–165.

Wallerstein, R. S., ed. (1981). *Becoming a Psychoanalyst: A Study of Psychoanalytic Supervision.* New York: Int. Univ. Press, pp. 227–268.

Wolkenfeld, F. (1984). The parallel process phenomenon revised: Some additional thoughts about the supervisory process. Paper delivered at Washington Square Institute, New York City, March 9, 1984.

40 East 89th Street, #14D
New York, N.Y. 10128

The Psychology of Powerlessness: Disorders of Self-Regulation and Interactional Regulation as a Newer Paradigm for Psychopathology

JAMES S. GROTSTEIN, M.D.

W HEN WE ATTEMPT TO UNDERSTAND psychopath- ology, we are confronted by two separate traditions or ap- proaches, that of psychoanalysis and that of empirical psychiatry. The basic assumptions of the former derive from the considerations of the vicissitudes of drives, manifested in a dynamic matrix of psy- chical conflict between those drives and nurturing objects that be- come enmeshed with them. The traditional psychoanalytic concep- tion of psychopathology seems based, consequently, on a theory of power. Empirical psychiatry, on the other hand, offers patholog- ical conceptions which implicate defects or deficiencies in psychical functioning, some of which may be inherited, others of which may develop in infancy and childhood. More recent contributions to psychoanalysis have complicated the seeming simplicity of this du- ality by suggesting a developmental deficit concept of psychic struc- ture harkening back to Freud's (1911) concept of decathexis. My contribution represents an attempt to formulate a psychoanalytic metapsychological umbrella that can integrate, not only the con-

Dr. Grotstein is Clinical Professor of Psychiatry at UCLA, Attending Staff Physician at Cedars-Sinai Medical Center, and Director of the Interdisciplinary Group for Advanced Studies in Primitive Mental States. This contribution is offered under the auspices of the latter.

flict (of power) and deficit (powerlessness) theories of psychoanalysis, but also integrate the two of them with the deficit theories which the findings of neurobiology are pressing upon psychoanalysis for integration.

Psychoanalysis seems to have emerged in a cultural milieu in which German Romanticism and Logical Positivism, succeeding Transcendentalism, imparted to that *Zeitgeist* a legacy of power that included Schopenhauer's *will* and Nietszche's "Superman." Freud translated this power motif into the concept of instinctual drives and founded his new science as the study of the distribution of and defense against this arcane power. Yet the concept of powerlessness had already begun to emerge with the contributions of Janet (see Strachey, 1974, p. 318) who considered hysteria to be due to a splitting of the personality secondary to an innate psychological weakness. Janet believed that all normal mental functions depended upon a capacity for synthesis, and that hysteria was due to a *maladie par faiblesse,* a "disease due to weakness." Freud (1911) himself, as stated above, dealt with the phenomenon of weakness when he considered decathexis as an ego defect in psychosis, a subject to be taken up by Freeman (1959, 1969, 1970) and Wexler (1971).

More recently, the concept of deficit psychology has reemerged in psychoanalytic theory, thanks to the contributions of Bibring (1953), Winnicott (1958, 1965), A. Reich (1960), Lichtenstein (1961), Bion (1962, 1963, 1965, 1970), Balint (1968), Bowlby (1969, 1973, 1980), Broucek (1979), and particularly Kohut (1971, 1977, 1978, 1984).

One of the first major papers after Freud that dealt with the importance of deficiency states was by Bibring (1953), who challenged Freud's (1917) explanatory hypothesis of melancholia by positing the primacy of ego weakness as opposed to Freud's view that depression was due to the repression of one's hostile feelings toward an object.

Bibring (1953) believed that depression was the emotional expression of a state of helplessness and powerlessness irrespective of what may have caused the breakdown of the mechanisms of self-esteem. Instead, he believed that depression resulted from a collapse of the ego's self-esteem. Bibring's work foreshadowed the development of the school of ego psychology in this country and the school of object relations in Great Britain, the developments from which introduced the importance of nurture (primarily the maternal object) as a major consideration in the infant's development. An important inference to be derived from the developments of these two schools was that of an ego deficiency secondary to disappointment in an object. The effect of the contributions of ego psychology were in no small measure to mitigate emphasis on the harsh impact of the power of the child's instincts and to stress, instead, the modifying factor of the environment as an adaptational, "cogwheeling" co-factor in development.

Winnicott (1958, 1965) addressed the issue of defective parenting from many perspectives. Principal among these were (a) the failure of the mother to give preoccupied maternal attention at a critical phase during infancy, (b) her failure to create a transitional relatedness with the infant, and (c) her impingement on her infant's privacy, thereby causing the infant to develop a false self in conformity with the mother and the environment in contrast to an inner, withdrawn true self.

Balint (1968) came forth with the important concept of the *basic fault* which had to do with the critical background quality that the failure of the early nurturing mother imparts to the child, leaving a legacy of permanent defectiveness, one which he felt was beyond the capacity of analysis to repair.

It is Bowlby (1969, 1973, 1980), however, to whom credit should be given for the most significant theory of powerlessness. Because of his pioneering work in attachment and his designation of pathological forms of attachment, I include his conceptualizations in my own schema so as to state, finally, that *all psychopathology constitutes primary or secondary disorders of bonding or attachment and manifests itself as disorders of self and/or interactional regulation.*

Broucek (1979), following in Bibring's footsteps, and those of Papoušek (1969; Papoušek and Papoušek, 1975), Watson (1972), and Bower (1977), emphasizes the importance of the infant's developing a sense of confidence in being able to protect his or her developing sense of self from the trauma of "failed influence over events which the infant expects on the basis of previous experience, to be able to 'cause' or predict" (p. 313). White (1959) called this phenomenon the pleasure of *competence* and the displeasure of incompetence in infant development.

Lynd's *Shame and the Sense of Identity* (1958) highlighted the importance of feelings of shame over behavioral failures and contrasted them with guilt, which was more reflective of aggression and hostility. Lynd pointed out that shame to its victim seemed to be unexpungable whereas guilt could be atoned for and was therefore modifiable.

Wurmser (1981) has also written on the phenomenon shame and links it with low self-esteem and failures of achievement. He details the various masks which it manifests, but he emphasizes that his concept of shame is "riveted to the premise of conflict" (p. 15).

The importance of the concept of deficit seems to have resurfaced recently from different points simultaneously. These include self psychology, studies on alexithymia, the revival of interest in the psychoanalytic treatment of borderline and narcissistic disorders, advances in the psychoanalytic conceptualization and treatment of infantile autistic and childhood psychotic disorders, and from revelations emanating from infant development studies. The concepts of self psychology which have been elaborated by Kohut (1971, 1977) and his followers postulate a psychoanalytic psychology predicated upon the primacy of defect rather than psychic conflict. They postulate that the defect is in the cohesion of the nuclear self because of a defectiveness in its constituency of selfobject support emanating from selfobject experiences in infancy and childhood. The self–selfobject relationships comprise a mirroring, an idealizing, a twinship, and a merger variety. Defects to self psychologists, therefore, would predicate the infant's failure to have internalized functions that are normally supplied by the parents. The deficiency concepts of self psychology were elaborated in attempts to understand the pathology of the narcissistic personality disorder, which they now call a disorder of the self.

Simultaneously, treatment problems with the borderline disorder came into prominence, and a debate began as to whether these patients were analyzable. Thanks to the contributions of Searles, Giovacchini, Boyer, Masterson and Rinsley, Sullivan, and others on this continent, as well as the Kleinian and British object relations groups in England, considerable progress has been made which warranted a positive verdict as to the analyzability of many cases of this disorder. While some analysts use conflict theory (Giovacchini and Boyer), others (Sullivan, Searles, and Masterson and Rinsley) utilize a deficiency model. Searles (1955, 1959, 1963) spoke of the efficiency of symbiotic relatedness in schizophrenic and borderline patients and also of their attempts to deal with psychosis in their parents. Masterson and Rinsley (1975) postulated a defect in borderlines, experienced most keenly at the rapprochement subphase of separation-individuation.

More recently, other analysts have emphasized defects in primitive mental disorders. Bick (1968) and Meltzer (1975) have formulated the concept of adhesive identity, a disorder that takes place in autistic psychotic children in the early postnatal period, the effect of which is the subjects' lack of feeling of having a skin boundary. They consequently adhere to object surfaces in order to get a temporary sense of identity. Meltzer links these children with Deutsch's (1942) "as-if" patients.

Tustin (1980, 1981a, b) formulates that there are two major kinds of psychotic children, the encapsulated type (infantile autistic psychosis proper) and the confusional type (childhood schizophrenia). Both types suffer from premature psychological birth, at-one-ment from the bonding object with the resultant precipitation of a premature "two-ness." These hapless children seem not to have a transitional bridge to the object and consequently become "autosensual," by which Tustin means that the infant's senses, which are normally the bridge to the object, no longer extend to the object, who is now experienced as being dangerously far away and alien.

Thus far I have emphasized intrapsychic dysregulation. Interactional dysregulation emerges in a variety of ways. The child's selfobject function already alluded to is to give cohesiveness, meaningfulness, and fulfillment to the parents and other siblings in a variety of family-regulatory functions normally. If the family belongs to a minority group or to a group that the larger culture has "appointed" as a "prey" subgroup for their "morally predatory" persecution, then the function of one or more of the children in a family may be that of the *hero* or *messiah,* the special and gifted one whose future victories and accomplishments remove the stigma of the family's shame. On a more practical basis, however, families dominated by parents who have marked psychopathology may often impose upon one child the role of hero or messiah and upon the other, as scapegoat, the one on whom they project their own sense of inadequacies and deficits. Often the role of hero or messiah *and* scapegoat are levied upon the same child. I have elsewhere (1986b) discussed the role of Oedipus as that of a human sacrifice, much like Christ, as a characteristic of families and cultures from the beginning of time — where the innocent child is to suffer in order to redeem the defaulted family or group.

In a parallel contribution, Epstein (1979) describes the unusually high statistical incidence of endogenous-like disorders in children of the Holocaust and postulates that the historic event was of such power as to behave almost as if it had given rise to a "cultural gene" (personal communication).

The concept of alexithymia has thrown additional light on deficiency states. Alexithymia refers to the state of "not knowing the name of one's feelings," thereby implicating nonrecognition of the very existence of feelings, which then leads to the somatization of putative emotions. The alexithymic therefore seems to relegate the body, as opposed to the mind, to experience the feelings substitutively as psychosomatic symptoms. Alexithymia has been explored in France by de M'Uzan (1974) and McDougall (1978, 1980), and in this country by Nemiah (1978), Sifneos (1973, 1975, 1977), Krystal (1979), Rickles (1981, 1983a, 1983b), Lesser (1981), Lesser et al. (1979), Lesser and Lesser (1983), and Taylor (1984, 1985). Hoppe (1977, 1978) has found that a syndrome like alexithymia seems to develop in persons subjected to overwhelming stress. The population he studied, concentration camp survivors, allegedly demonstrated a secondary form of alexithymia, which Hoppe suggests was due to a veritable functional commissurotomy of the corpus callosum, which unites the two cerebral hemispheres. The teleological purpose suggested by Hoppe for this commissurotomy was that the alexithymia results from the need to inconsequentialize the significance, and therefore the emotional pain, of the overwhelming experience.

Alexithymia serves as a bridge to the "actual neurosis" first formulated by Freud (1895, 1898) and recently reviewed by Gediman (1983, 1984) and Kaplan (1984). The "actual neurosis" implies the contentless state of the pure, untransformed instincts. Gediman states:

A comprehensive and unitary psychoanalytic approach must acknowledge the importance of the so-called "contentless mental state" of mounting psychic tensions. . . . Once these states are endowed with meaning through free associations and the joint constructive efforts of analyst and analysand, they may also be drawn into the orbit of neurotic conflict, if they have not already been drawn in by the patient alone, and then they may be dealt with analytically in connexion with the components of compromise formations which have interpretable meaning [1984, p. 200].

Both Gediman and Kaplan offer a separate and a unified status for the "actual neurosis" with the psychoneuroses. The "actual neurosis" first discussed by Freud (1895, 1898) implies the contentlessness state of pure, untransformed instinctual energy and can be correlated with annihilation anxiety or organismic panic (Greenacre, 1967; Jacobson, 1971). This state, also referred to as the *traumatic state,* has many similarities to the psychotic states of mania and of schizophrenia and has always been viewed in terms of its overwhelming power over the ego. It is my contention that this primitive state of panic represents a state of powerlessness, not only of the ego's capacity to regulate it, but also of the id's capacity to mythify it into dreams or phantasies. As such, the "actual neurosis," or the panic syndrome generally, represents a state of powerlessness of the psyche to withstand or to transform the data it experiences into meaningful psychical elements via primary or secondary process.

Bion (1962, 1963, 1965, 1970) has dealt with this phenomenon as a defect of alpha function — which he defines as the normal person's capacity to receive sensory data and to allow it to be experienced by encoding it with attributes, significance, and meaning — and posits that it is the absence of this function which characterizes psychosis. *I extend Bion's concept of defective or absent alpha function in psychosis to postulate that the latter constitutes not only an ego defect, as has commonly been thought, but also an id defect; that is, the psychotic does not have sufficient functioning of primary process to transform the data of personal experience into dreams, phantasies, or personal myths — only into hallucinations or delusions, which are the failures of phantasies and dreams.*

Within recent years, a plethora of data and formulations have emerged independently from sociobiology, infant development, and neurobiology, especially brain research on bilaterality and neurocognitive and neurotransmittor dysfunctions in a variety of emotional disorders. The data and formulations are of such importance as to demand the attention of psychoanalytic theorists and practitioners and seem to herald the advent of an interdisciplinary future for psychoanalytic theory and practice. Ostow (1962, 1970, 1979, 1986) has attempted to bring psychoanalysis into alignment with psychopharmacological research and with attachment theory, and Kafka (1984) has done similarly with neurocognitive disorders.

The psychiatric literature has also brought forth descriptive concepts of deficiencies in borderline states. Andrulonis et al. (1981, 1982) have characterized a form of borderline psychopathology other than purely organic or psychological as having dyslexia, learning difficulties, and attention-deficit disorders. Meanwhile, contributors from the field of psychobiology, such as Wender and Klein (1981), Akiskal (1983), and others, have postulated that the borderline state may be a misnomer and may be more properly seen as a variant of affective disorders in which a biological deficiency state exists that is neurochemical in nature, the psychological consequences of which are purely secondary. The aspects of defectiveness that can be applied to the borderline from these descriptive studies on affective disorders can be thought of as follows: many patients may suffer from (a) an inherited bipolar disorder, (b) a unipolar disorder (either manic or depressive), (c) a cyclothymic disorder – less severe than (a) but more severe than (d) a dysthymic disorder (which is today's term for what used to be called neurotic depression). Further, the depressive syndrome or hypomanic syndrome may occur cyclically as an altered state in an otherwise normal personality and/or in an abnormal personality which may have become characterized either as hypomanic or as depressed in an ego-syntonic manner, whereas the state would be ego-dystonic.

The psychobiological contributions to the concept of defects are of signal importance to psychoanalysis generally and to the treatment of borderlines specifically for a variety of reasons, but the main one is the interpenetration of the personality by a psychical disorder. Whereas psychobiologists say the biochemical aspects of the disorder are primary, I have hypothesized (1984a, b) that psychosis generally may be due to a psychosomatic disorder of the central nervous system, which may at times be secondary to the traumatic alteration of neurophysiological functions by the advent of overinclusion of stimuli, which in turn may be due to a defective threshold barrier, of either hereditary or environmental origin. It is also probable, however, that primary hereditary defects of a neuro-perceptual-cognitive-affective nature may occur so as to alter the individual's capacity to regulate moods.

Psychobiological contributions to the literature on deficits include neuroanatomic, neurochemical, neurophysiological, and neuropsychological. Elliot (1978) has written on the neuropsychological aspects of antisocial behavior in the psychopath and has found a significant degree of prefrontal deficit in them. A vast wealth of material from psychopharmacology has suggested the high probability that many mental disorders are inheritable. Among these are the disorders of the schizophrenic spectrum and the affective disorders, including depression, cyclothymia, hypomania, and mania. It has also been demonstrated that the Briquet syndrome, alcoholism, and sociopathy may not only be inheritable illnesses, but, as tendencies, occupy the same genetic locus on the chromosome.

The concept of endogenous affective illness is, however, misleading. Students of affective disorders generally understand "endogenousness' to predicate the family inheritance of a predisposition or to a vulnerability to the expression of this illness complex, but a newer meaning seems to be emerging which places the concept of endogenousness in a state of ambiguity. The second meaning is that the significant experience of object loss from the fetal stage through infancy and early childhood may also predispose one to being at risk for affective illness. As stated earlier, studies of Holocaust survivors and their children seem to support this second definition (Epstein, 1980, 1982). What seems to emerge, therefore, is the probability that serious dysthymic, cyclothymic, and major unipolar and bipolar illness may be a somatopsychic and/or a psychosomatic illness in which the central nervous system seems to be deeply involved in terms of the alterations in the production and/or uptake of key neurotransmittors, particularly serotonin and/or norepinephrine (Wender & Klein, 1981).

Psychopathology Reformulated as Disorders of Self and Interactional Regulation

I am here making a plea for acknowledging the importance of a significantly different track of psychopathogenesis. I am proposing that the patient's experience of being defective, is due not only to the experience of instinctual drives, their vicissitudes, and the defenses the ego must direct against them, but also to the primacy of the experience of defectiveness, whether this defectiveness is constitutional-hereditary-congenital or acquired through defective bonding from the would-be nurturing environment. I use the term *defect* when its more traditional or historic psychoanalytic meaning is indicated (such as in "ego defect"), and *deficit* when referring to its usage in (a) self psychology, as a failure in the development of function of the self, and (b) neuropsychological parlance wherein deficit connotes a failure of function that may be due to a reversible breakdown in neurocognitive organization. In the latter case, an irreversible breakdown or failure of function to develop may be due to a *"defect"* having an altered anatomical substrate. Room must also be left for the concept of *deficiency,* however, which has biopsychosocial implications and connotes reversibility. All three comprise the parameters of *powerlessness.* The concept I am advocating generalizes and extends the contributions of Janet, Winnicott, Balint, Bion, A. Reich, as well as Kohut and his followers. This concept of disorders of self-regulation includes and transcends the work of the aforementioned writers by including biopsychosocial perspectives so as to achieve an interdisciplinary integration for psychoanalytic theory. In brief, I advocate a psychopathology of powerlessness as an alternative to the classical psychoanalytic concept of instinctual conflict, and I choose the concept of self-regulation (and interactional regulation) as a vehicle to embrace this psychology of powerlessness.

I posit a concept of self-regulation (or self-modulation) in which the hapless patient consciously and/or unconsciously experiences his or her limitations as defects (deficits or deficiencies) and consequently conducts his or her life in a manner that militates against the irruptive expression of these weaknesses, whose epiphany seems inevitable as the patient inexorably ascends the maturational ladder of life with its progressive responsibilities and demands, with the consequence of ultimate jeopardy because of the fear of the evocation of the appearance of these deficits.

In furthering the application of an alternative perspective to psychoanalytic theory and clinical phenomena, I also propose here, as I have elsewhere (1984a, b; 1985a, b), that the ego and the id, as well as the superego, constitute complementary and therefore alternatively functioning entities. One of the immediate consequences of this intervention would be to consider that the instinctual drives, rather than being the *source* of mental activity, are basic *regulators* of impactful existential moments working side by side with secondary process in order to give personal meaning as well as personal solace to the data of these personal experiences. Another consequence would be to consider repression and the ego's mechanisms of defense derived from it to function as a psychic regulatory membrane which interfaces two psychical domains and therefore functions in a Janus-like manner rather than in a unilateral direction. In other words, the so-called repressive barrier is a twoway membrane that functions to protect the domain of the id from the ego just as much as to protect the ego from the id. It is more a modulator than censor.

I propose the term *disorders of self-regulation* to encompass the concept of a schema of psychopathology that addresses the twofold aspect of defect-deficit-deficiency theory in the following ways: (1) The self is comprised of a *hierarchy of states* (arousal, concentration, attention, information-processing, self-esteem, sleep, wakefulness, affects, needs, etc.) which fall into dysregulation because of the failure of inherent internal control-regulators and/or external object and selfobject modulators. (2) These dysregulated states cause alarm or tension and threaten catastrophe to the organism and consequently precipitate the emergence of symptoms which either directly reflect this alarm (anxiety, panic, the traumatic state, depression, etc.) or seem to screen it via secondary symptoms which offer a makeshift "floor" under, or container around, what Kohut (1971) calls a fragmenting self so as to protect it from disintegrating catastrophe.

I propose, consequently, that the most fundamental unregulated (and/or dysregulated) portion of the psyche is constituted, not by instinctual drives (because they too are regulators on par with ego structures), but instead by the experience of randomness, meaninglessness, catastrophe, dissolution, "nameless dread," the "void," etc., and that the ego and the id attempt to regulate or modulate this meaninglessness by assigning "realistic" *and* imaginal meaningfulness to it. If the primitive experience is one of meaninglessness or chaos, then the first attempts to organize this experience into meaningfulness would be that of primary process in attempting to mythify this chaos into what Klein (1945) terms persecutory anxiety in a phantasmal cosmos comprised of polarized and polarizing demons. The failure of the paranoid-schizoid position to organize this chaos results in its devolving phenomenologically into psychotic fragmentation, or, later, as the depressive position is approximated, into phantasies of "black holes" or of mutilation, of being "ripped" or "torn" by the pulling away of mother's body, etc.

The threshold barrier to the emergence of this meaninglessness or chaos is lowered by (a) the absence of selfobject and object support, (b) the experience of defects-deficits-deficiencies in the neuro-perceptual-affective-cognitive-behavioral modalities either inherently, congenitally, or by virtue of the impact of a depriving or impinging "nurture" on the developmental agenda.

Mental symptoms, consequently, are not merely the result of psychodynamic conflict but are also attempts to restore balance to a critically imbalanced psyche. I therefore extend Gediman's (1983, 1984) concept of the "actual neurosis" and its relationship to psychoneurosis to the following hypothesis: the "actual neurosis" (primary meaninglessness) and the infantile neurosis (primary archaic meaningfulness) exist in a dialectical relationship in all people from the very beginning. Inherent and acquired psychobiological disorders of the central nervous system highlight the former and thereby impose on the latter the task of psychical regulation. Depressive patients in particular emphasize this "balancing" trend when they compulsively seek aerobics and other physical enterprises, some of which may be dangerous. Danger, like aerobics, seems to stimulate the hypothalamo-pituitary-adrenal axis into releasing noradrenalin, ACTH, enkephalines, endomorphins, etc., all of which alleviate depressive symptoms. As such, these symptoms, including phobias, gambling, obsessive-compulsive traits, compulsive hyperactivity personalities, sadomasochism, and so many others, can be thought of, not only in terms of their individual psychodynamic meanings, but also as manic defenses (Klein, 1945) against the heightened specter of catastrophe which vulnerability to depres-

sion, panic, etc., imposes on its victims — and similarly for patients
with substance abuse who choose the agent they need to regulate
their dysregulated state.

The deficits associated with depression, for instance, can be: (a)
purely psychological; (b) biological but not currently psychological; (c) separate — a psychological depression independent of a biological depression; and (d) mixed. Depression generally, and the
mixed form in particular, can be demonstrated to be either somatopsychic or psychosomatic or even both. That is, depression may
originate a somatic potentiality which can be triggered by an external event into a frank depression, and/or a primary psychical depression can have such impact on the soma that it secondarily
causes a corresponding alteration of the central nervous system
substrate. Some of these depressive psychosomatic disorders are reversible either spontaneously or via psychotherapy and psychoanalysis, whereas others may be partially reversible, and still others,
perhaps the main part of those which are somatopsychic, not at all.

Borderline disorders may have the following deficits: (A) borderline personality *trait* disturbances which include any of the spectrum of cognitive deficits, affect-regulation deficits, and be-
havioral-regulation deficits manifested as: (1) disorders of self-
esteem regulation, (2) disorders of affect regulation, (3) disorders
of attention and concentration (gating and information pro-
cessing), (4) disorders of planning, and (5) disorders of behavior;
(B) interpenetration of personality trait by an affect-state disrup-
tion, including cyclothymia, major unipolar and bipolar disorders,
and/or panic. Thus, the borderline may have a wide spectrum of
deficits ranging from the neurocognitive through the endogenous
to the psychological. In the psychoanalytic psychotherapy of these
disorders, close attention must be paid to the detailing of as many
of these defects and/or deficits and/or deficiencies as possible so as
to separate them off from the feeling self, and then to name them,
"walk around them," so to speak, and make them an integral part of
the patient's understanding of him or herself as a handicapping
entity so that ultimately the patient can either allow them to be

healed and/or be "subtracted from the equation" of his or her sensitivity to experience.

Interactional Regulation

I believe that Kohut's (1971) formulations, referred to earlier, following as they did in the footsteps of A. Reich's (1960) concept of self-esteem regulation in narcissism, offer formulations that allow for a broader extension of the concept of self-regulation beyond the newer concept of self-disorders. Insofar as Kohut's formulations hypothesize an independent development of the self vis-á-vis its relationship to objects, we now have a whole new way of conceiving of human motivation and psychopathology along lines first adumbrated by Freud (1907, 1908, 1910, 1912, 1913). More specifically, Freud speculated that the libidinal instincts were counterposed to the ego instincts, the latter being directed toward the preservation of the self and the former toward the preservation of the race. Freud (1914) later abandoned this distinction when he reformulated that the ego itself is the id's first object, and therefore the self-preservative instincts of the ego are subordinated to the sexual drives of the id *ipso facto*. He was subsequently to arrive at yet another dialectical dichotomy, that between the life instinct and the death instinct (Freud, 1920).

I should like to rescue Freud's original hypothesis from the shadows into which he long ago retired it and amalgamate it with Kohut's (1971) theory of the duality of developmental agendas of the self — which he, too, later abandoned in favor of a hegemony of the development of the self over the development of its relationships to objects (Kohut, 1977) — and offer a theory which speculates that each human organism, like its other primate analogues, is motivated toward *self-preservation* and toward *group preservation* via *innate altruism* — provided that there is sufficiently intact bonding or attachment to a group unit (Lumsden & Wilson, 1983; see Alper, 1985).

Further, I consider Kohut's selfobject concept to occupy an interactional position of mutuality between child and parent so that not only do parents normally serve selfobject functions for their child, but the latter normally serves selfobject functions for the parents, especially in terms of guaranteeing family-clan-racial survival and also sources of meaningfulness and completeness for the parents. Children may also serve abnormal selfobject functions for their parents (Searles, 1959; Wynne, 1968, 1969; Stierlin, 1972, 1973; Masterson & Rinsley, 1975; Rinsley, 1977; Masterson, 1981).

Self-Regulation and Interactional Regulation as Dialectics

With the above as the theoretical basis, I speculate that the human being develops, normally or abnormally, along the axis of *self-regulation,* on one hand, and along the axis of *interactional regulation,* on the other. Freud's (1920) concept of a "stimulus barrier" contains the idea of the existence of an inborn threshold to perceptual stimulation and other excitation. He conceived of it as the precursor to the development of the ego defense mechanisms, thereby viewing it as defending against instinctual drives from within the organism and from impinging stimuli outside the organism. Further, he postulated two forms of stimulus barriers: (a) a constitutional threshold for all incoming stimuli as a protective mechanisms against flooding, and (b) the maternal reinforcement of the barrier. Benjamin (1965), following upon Freud's concept of the barrier, suggested that the infant could be an active participant in barrier regulation through its evocative gestures to its mother. Gediman (1971, 1983, 1984) broadened the concept of the stimulus barrier by suggesting the concept of "barrier hunger," wherein she suggested the need for the barrier to be "toned" in order to function optimally. Even though Stern (1977, 1983), has discredited the value of the concept of the stimulus barrier in the infant, I nevertheless believe it has heuristic value in describing a two-way membrane which, like the cell membrane, acts as an active interface between two domains, the domain of the internal world and the domain of external reality, and it is the forerunner not only of the ego's defense mechanisms but also of the function of the skin boundary itself.

I thus postulate that the so-called ego defense mechanisms are really inter- and intrapsychical regulatory or modulatory mechanisms which modulate the emotional, instinctual, and affective traffic of information traveling into and out of the psyche and between agencies of the psyche. As I have said elsewhere (1986a), I believe primary process and secondary process are parallel and complementary functions which process the data of emotional and reality experience from two different points and then "stereoscopize" these various data-gathering perspectives into a larger perspective. Thus, by following this logic, the phenomenon of repression can be seen as a hypothetical membrane between two domains which allows for the mutual regulation and toning of each by the other, much as in a tennis match where each player, though pragmatically oppositional, is really bettering the game of the other and keeping it in optimum functioning.

My postulation is that psychopathology constitutes a breakdown in one or more of these regulatory functions, resulting in the development of a temporary chaotic dysregulation, which is then succeeded, failing normal restitution, by a more nearly permanent pathological regulation. Thus symptoms do not regulate instinctual drives, but rather, instinctual drives, among other psychical entities, attempt to regulate more basic states of the psyche such as chaos, anxiety, depression, catastrophe, all of which constitute negative states — or states of acute chronic deficits. The apparent flooding of the psyche by what seem to be instinctual drive derivatives signifies, if my theory is correct, catastrophe.

Achieving regulatory effectiveness involves the activation and coordination of complex, inborn, and culturally derived systems of reciprocal communication and mutual adaptation between infant and mother, concepts which have been subsumed under Bowlby's (1969, 1973, 1980) theory of bonding and attachment, which have been modified by Hofer's (1975, 1981) concept of specific systems of regulation, and Thomas and Chess' (1980, 1982) concept of the

"goodness of fit." Thus, a defective inherent capacity for stimulus-
barrier regulation may be one of the constitutional legacies which
predisposes an infant to schizophrenic illness—in addition to an
alternative and/or additional set of risk factors, the inherent temperament, the maternal environment, and the goodness of fit, all of
which contribute to the intactness or deficiency of the bonding, attachment, and specific systems regulation (Hofer, 1975, 1981).

My thesis is that all symptom complexes can now be seen in two
ways in tandem: (a) as mental and emotional disturbances involving
a breakdown in primary states of self-regulation, and (b) as secondary states, known as symptoms, syndromes, etc., following in train
as attempts to re-establish an altered form of self-regulation
(and/or interactional regulation)—and, failing that, becoming
symptom complexes which "announce" or "proclaim" the distressed state.

Discussion

The following vignette should demonstrate many of the salient issues of disorders of self-regulation and of interactional regulation.

M. R. is a 41-year-old attorney who consulted me following previous psychotherapeutic ventures, with minimal gain, for impotence. At the time of consultation, he had been married for seven
years, had a five-year-old son, and dated the impotence to the birth
of his son. He was the eldest of three children, having two younger
sisters. His mother and father divorced when he was ten. Father was
known to have suffered from a manic-depressive psychosis and
took Lithium periodically. The patient did not have a good relationship with his father due largely to the latter's "touchiness" and
need to be placated when he was moody. Father had been orphaned
by the death of both parents when he was in his infancy and was
raised by an older brother. Mother was the eldest of three sisters,
was less loved than the others, she believed, but was the most de-

voted to her father. The patient was more devoted to his own son, he claimed, than was his wife.

The above themes and many others emerged in the first three years of the analysis so that we were able, from the transference neurosis, to reconstruct intelligible and incredible themes of a highly sensitive, withdrawn child who had been intimidated by having been left as the "little man" in a household of three women by the father's leaving, of a yearning for a real father who could help him, advise him, and nurture him into adulthood to give him permission for sexual potency, etc. It also began to emerge that the patient experienced a restricted mental life. He dreamed sparingly, suffered from anhedonia, did not have restful sleep, and seemed to be obsessive in his thought processes and compulsive in his daily habits. He constructed large lists for daily activities in his personal and professional life which he adhered to with unusual punctiliousness. He often said that, although he does not enjoy his work, he misses it when he is home on weekends. It also became apparent that he served as a "hero selfobject" to his sisters and his mother but regrets that he was never able to make his father feel better.

Interpretations addressing the above childhood themes, whether in terms of psychical conflict or of selfobject deficiency, seemed to have minimal effect on this patient for the first three years of the analysis when he was on the couch. Finally, he spontaneously got up from the couch and sat in the chair, telling me that he never liked being on the couch, felt distant from me, and felt "kind of numb." I finally was able to see another picture beginning to emerge side by side with the infantile-childhood neurosis and from ambivalent feelings toward his wife. His sense of numbness, anhedonia, fitful sleep, and obsessive-compulsiveness suggested an endogenous affective disorder which was inherited from his father. I postulated that this affective disorder had been characterized by a lifelong experience of hypersensitivity to interpersonal disappointments and had caused him to hypercompensate for feelings of defectiveness by compulsively working overstrenuously in order to accomplish his life goals. His "Type-A Personality" began to emerge as a way of regulating his sense of deficiency, as did his compulsive work habits. His experience of isolation and withdrawal from others was a way of protecting himself from the exposure of his deficit.

When I sent him for psychopharmacological consultation, the consultant performed a Dexamethasone Suppression Test for cortical secretion, which turned out to be significantly abnormal. The consultant then placed the patient on Imipramine medication. The results were dramatic, far-reaching, and sustaining up to and through the present time. The analysis took on a dramatic new course. The patient regained his potency, was amazed at how much he was now beginning to enjoy activities, felt more refreshed when he awoke from sleep, and believed he had a "new lease on life." One interesting example of his change is revealed in the following vignette: "You know, I never wanted to tell you this, but I never liked that picture hanging over your desk which I had to stare at all the time I was lying down. The water looked cold and forboding, and the islands in it were stark, barren, and isolated. Now I think the picture is very inviting. I see a very warm orange-colored island in the background and the water seems to be beckoning."

In using this case for explication, I do not mean to imply that all cases of deficit should be subjected to psychopharmacological treatment. Many cases of defect or deficit, although they may be endogenous and therefore biochemical entities, may *not* be treatable psychopharmacologically and, furthermore, most patients (and particularly most therapists) prefer to try the strictly analytic approach in favor of "getting help from a friend." Besides, the state of pharmacologic efficacy is not such that pharmaceuticals can satisfactorily address the whole span of these disorders. I am suggesting, however, that the therapist keep in mind the possibility of a second theme, that of the importance of defect-deficit-deficiency in all its ramifications so that the therapist and the patient can then survey the nature of the deficit, name it, and realize its impact on the development of the personality. Depressive numbness in a child may trivialize otherwise adequate parental ministrations to that child so that the child may later reveal in the analysis that mother and father were never much caring or were inadequate, etc., whereas it was the depressive barrier of numbness that interfered with the interaction. The same can be true in the reverse where mother and/or father can suffer from either hyper-irritability and/or numbness, both legacies of an endogenous manic-depressive or depressive disorder. The aforementioned patient began to feel differently about his parents' relationship to him when he was able to understand that his mother suffered from an endogenous depressive illness and his father from a frank, manic-depressive illness which had been barely regulated by lithium.

Type-A Personality (and the patient I decribed characterized himself as such) has often been linked with alexithymia (McDougall, 1978, 1980) but can also be seen as having an endogenous deficit disorder. The hyperactivity and emphasis on action in general seem to comprise a compulsive defense, often hypomanic in nature, which attempts to create an artificial "floor" over the inner experience of deficit, behind which is the experience of a depressive "hole" or panicky chaos. This sense of "floorlessness" or of "inner chaos" or of "holes in the psyche" seems to be the legacy of most patients with endogenous disorders, some of whom exclaim, "Now I have a floor!" (or a variant thereof) when they are effectively treated by antidepressant or anti-anxiety medication. The abovementioned patient one day exclaimed with delight, "So this is what it is like to have a floor!"

In brief, I posit that there are a wide number of affective disorders ranging from the dysthymic, cyclothymic, through major unipolar and bipolar disorders which manifest themselves as disorders of dysregulation due to depression, excessive cycling, hypomania, panic, and a tendency toward somatization and pain. Perhaps all patients feeling depression, for instance, will also have somatic manifestations to one degree or another. Whether or not the biological correlate of the depression is of primary importance or merely an accessory somatic "spill-over" from the psychical is a matter for the clinician to determine. Some depressions seem primarily psychobiological whereas others seem primarily psychical, and the treatment rationale follows accordingly.

114   JAMES S. GROTSTEIN

The Severe Superego as a Self-Regulatory Entity

Space does not permit me to detail the analysis of my patient's severe superego. Suffice it to say that I initially understood his impotence and the general restrictedness of his life as due to his victimi-
zation by a severe superego, which owed its origin not only to the
model of his disapproving, distant, unloving, and unavailable father but also to the introjection of the projective identifications of
his own hostile and ambivalent feelings toward his key objects.
What finally began to emerge from the analysis following the
employment of medication was the incredible observation that his
severe superego seemed to a large measure to be "soluble" in
Imipramine. In other words, the severity of his superego was due,
as Bibring (1953) long ago adumbrated, to a need to achieve order
and integration in a psyche beset by panic, chaos, or depressive
hopelessness. I have found the same to be true in other cases as well.
    Ultimately, as I have already said, the ego's defense mechanisms
are erected, not against drives per se, but against chaos or randomness, which are existentially experienced as *meaninglessness*. The
superego, although generally cast as the anatagonist in most psychical scenarios in analysis, constitutes a source of strength, of godlike
opinions. Even in its severity, the superego gives meaningfulness
and order to its subject, the patient, much as the severe Yaweh did
for the children of Israel long ago.

REFERENCES

Akiskal, H. S. (1983). Dysthymic disorder: Psychopathology and proposed chronic depres-
    sive subtypes. *Amer. J. Psychiat.*, 140:11-20.
Alper, J. (1985). The roots of morality. *Science 85*, 6:70-77.
Andrulonis, P. A., Glueck, B. C., Strobel, C. F., & Vogel, N. (1982). Borderline personality
    subcategories. *J. Nerv. Ment. Dis.*, 170:670-679.
—————— —————— et al. (1981). Organic brain dysfunction and the borderline syndrome.
    Psychiat. Clin. N. Amer., 4:47-66.
Balint, M. (1968). *The Basic Fault.* London: Tavistock.
Benjamin, J. D. (1965). Developmental biology and psychoanalysis. In *Psychoanalysis and
    Current Biological Thought*, ed. N. Greenfield & W. Lewis. Madison & Milwaukee,
    Madison, Wisc.: Univ. Wisconsin Press, pp. 57-70.
Bibring, E. (1953). The mechanism of depression. In *Affective Disorders*, ed. P. Greenacre.
    New York: Int. Univ. Press, pp. 13-48.

Bick, E. (1968). The experience of the skin in early object relations. *Int. J. Psychoanal.*, 49:484-486.

Bion, W. R. (1962). *Learning from Experience.* New York: Basic Books.

———— (1963). *Elements of Psychoanalysis.* New York: Basic Books.

———— (1965). *Transformation.* New York: Basic Books.

———— (1970). *Attention and Interpretation.* New York: Basic Books.

Bower, T. G. R. (1977). *A Primer of Infant Development.* San Francisco: W. H. Freeman.

Bowlby, J. (1969). *Attachment and Loss, vol. I: Attachment.* New York: Basic Books.

———— (1973). *Attachment and Loss, vol. II: Separation.* New York: Basic Books.

———— (1980). *Attachment and Loss, vol. III: Loss.* New York: Basic Books.

Broucek, F. (1979). Efficacy in infancy: A review of some experimental studies and their possible implications for clinical theory. *Int. J. Psychoanal.*, 60:311-316.

De M'Uzan, M. (1974). Psychodynamic mechanisms in psychosomatic symptoms formation. *Psychother. and Psychosom.*, 23:103-110.

Deutsch, H. (1942). Some forms of emotional disturbance and their relationship to schizophrenia. *Psychoanal. Q.*, 11:301-321.

Elliot, S. A. (1978). Neurological aspects of antisocial behavior in the psychopath. In *A Comprehensive Study of Antisocial Disorders and Behaviors*, ed. W. H. Reed. New York: Brunner/Mazel, pp. 146-189.

Epstein, A. W. (1979). *Children of the Holocaust.* New York: Putnam.

———— (1980). Familial imperative ideas and actions. How encoded? *Biological Psychiat.*, 15:489-494.

———— (1982). Mental phenomena across generations: The Holocaust. *J. Amer. Acad. Psychoanal.*, 10:565-570.

Freeman, T. (1959). Aspects of defence in neurosis and psychosis. *Int. J. Psychoanal.*, 40:199-212.

———— (1969). *Psychopathology of the Psychoses.* New York: Int. Univ. Press.

———— (1970). The psychopathology of the psychoses: A reply to Arlow and Brenner. *Int. J. Psychoanal.*, 51:407-415.

Freud, S. (1895). On the grounds for detaching a particular syndrome from neurasthenia under the description 'anxiety neurosis.' *S.E.*, 3.

———— (1898). The sexuality in the aetiology of the neuroses. *S.E.*, 3.

———— (1907). Obsessive actions and religious practices. *S.E.*, 9.

———— (1908). On the sexual theories of children. *S.E.*, 9.

———— (1910). The psycho-analytic view of psychogenic disturbance of vision. *S.E.*, 11.

———— (1911). Psychoanalytic notes on an autobiographical account of a case of paranoia (dementia praecox). *S.E.*, 12.

———— (1912). On the universal tendency to debasement in the sphere of love (contributions to the psychology of love, II). *S.E.*, 11.

———— (1913). The claims of psycho-analysis to scientific interest. *S.E.*, 13.

———— (1914). On narcissism: An introduction. *S.E.*, 14.

———— (1920). *Beyond the pleasure principle. S.E.*, 18.

Gediman, H. K. (1971). The concept of stimulus barrier: Its review and reformulation as an adaptive ego function. *Int. J. Psychoanal.*, 52:243-257.

———— (1983). Annihilation anxiety: The experience of deficit in neurotic compromise formation. *Int. J. Psychoanal.*, 64:59-70.

———— (1984). Actual neurosis and psychoneurosis. *Int. J. Psychoanal.*, 65:191-202.

Greenacre, P. (1967). The influence of infantile trauma on genetic passions. In *Emotional Growth.* New York: Int. Univ. Press, 1971, pp. 260-299.

Grotstein, J. S. (1984a). A proposed revision of the psychoanalytic concept of primitive mental states: II. The borderline syndrome—Section 1: Disorders of autistic safety and symbiotic relatedness. *Contemp. Psychoanal.*, 19:570-604.

_____ (1984b). A proposed revision of the psychoanalytic concept of primitive mental states: II. The borderline syndrome—Section 2: The phenomenology of the borderline syndrome. *Contemp. Psychoanal.*, 20:77-119.

_____ (1984c). A proposed revision of the psychoanalytic concept of primitive mental states: II. The borderline syndrome—Section 3: The phenomenology of narcissistic disorders. *Contemp. Psychoanal.*, 20:266-343.

_____ (1986a). The dual-track theorem. Unpublished.

_____ (1986b). The sins of the fathers: A proposed revision of the psychoanalytic concept of the Oedipus complex. Unpublished.

Hofer, M. A. (1975). Infant separation responses and the maternal role. *Biological Psychiat.*, 10:149-153.

_____ (1981). Toward a developmental basis for disease predisposition: The effects of early maternal separation on brain, behavior, and cardiovascular system. In *Brain, Behavior, and Bodily Disease*, ed. H. Weiner, M. A. Hofer & A. J. Stunkard. New York: Raven Press, pp. 209-228.

Hoppe, K. D. (1977). Split brains in psychoanalysis. *Psychoanal. Q.*, 46:224-244.

_____ (1978). Split-brain—psychoanalytic findings and hypotheses. *J. Amer. Acad. Psychoanal.*, 6(2):193-213.

Jacobson, E. (1971). *Depression*. New York: Int. Univ. Press.

Kafka, E. (1984). Cognitive difficulties in psychoanalysis. *Psychoanal. Q.*, 53:533-550.

Kaplan, D. (1984). Some conceptual and technical aspects of the actual neurosis. *Int. J. Psychoanal.*, 65:295-306.

Klein, M. (1945). The Oedipus complex in the light of early anxieties. In *Contributions to Psycho-Analysis, 1921-1945*. London: Hogarth Press, 1948, pp. 339-390.

Kohut, H. (1971). *The Analysis of the Self*. New York: Int. Univ. Press.

_____ (1977). *The Restoration of the Self*. New York: Int. Univ. Press.

_____ (1978). *The Search for the Self*. New York: Int. Univ. Press.

_____ (1984). *How Does Analysis Cure?* Chicago: Univ. Chicago Press.

Krystal, H. (1979). Alexithymia and psychotherapy. *Amer. J. Psychother.*, 33:17-31.

Lesser, I. M. (1981). A review of the alexithymia concept. *Psychosom. Med.*, 43:531-543.

_____ Friedmann, C. T. H. & Ford, C. (1979). Alexithymia in somatizing patients. *Gen. Hosp. Psychiat.*, 1:256-261.

_____ & Lesser, B. Z. (1983). Alexithymia: Examining the development of a psychological concept. *Amer. J. Psychiat.*, 140:1305-1308.

Lichtenstein, H. (1961). Identity and sexuality. *J. Amer. Psychoanal. Assn.*, 9:179-260.

Lumsden, C. J. & Wilson, E. O. (1983). *Promethean Fire: Reflections on the Origin of Mind*. Cambridge, Ma.: Harvard Univ. Press.

Lynd, H. M. (1958). *On Shame and the Search for Identity*. New York: Harcourt Brace.

Masterson, J. (1981). *The Narcissistic and Borderline Disorders*. New York: Brunner/Mazel.

_____ & Rinsley, D. B. (1975). The borderline syndrome: The role of the mother in the genesis and the psychic structure of the borderline personality. *Int. J. Psychoanal.*, 56:163-177.

McDougall, J. (1978). *Plea for a Measure of Abnormality*. New York: Int. Univ. Press.

_____ (1980). A child is being eaten. *Contemp. Psychoanal.*, 1:417-459.

Meltzer, D. (1975). Adhesive identification. *Contemp. Psychoanal.*, 11:289-310.

Nemiah, J. (1978). Alexithymia and psychosomatic illness. *J. Clin. Exper. Psychiat.*, 39:25-37.

Ostow, M. (1962). *Drugs in Psychoanalysis and Psychotherapy.* New York: Basic Books.
_____ (1970). *The Psychology of Melancholy.* New York: Harper & Row.
_____ (1979), ed. *The Psychodynamic Approach to Drug Therapy.* New York: Psychoanalytic Research and Development Fund.
_____ (1986). Comments on the pathogenesis of the borderline disorder. In *The Borderline Patient: Emerging Concepts in Diagnosis, Psychodynamics, and Treatment,* ed. J. S. Grotstein, J. Lang, & M. Solomon. Hillsdale, N.J.: Analytic Press. In press.
Papoušek, H. (1969). Individual variability in learned response in human infants. In *Brain and Early Behavior,* ed. R. J. Robinson. London: Academic Press, pp. 251-263.
_____ & Papoušek, M. (1975). Cognitive aspects of preverbal social interaction between human infants and adults. CIBA Foundation Symposium. *Parent-Infant Interactions.* New York: Associated Scientific Publications, pp. 241-260.
Reich, A. (1960). Pathological forms of self-esteem regulation. *Psychoanal. Study Child,* 15:215-232.
Rickles, W. H. (1981). Biofeedback therapy and transitional phenomena. *Psychiat. Ann.,* 11:23-41.
_____ (1983a). Personality characteristics of psychosomatic patients. In *Biofeedback and Family Medical Practice,* ed. W. H. Rickles et al. New York: Plenum Press, pp. 155-174.
_____ (1983b). Self psychology and somatization: An integration with alexithymia. Presented to the Sixth Annual Conference of Self Psychology. Los Angeles, California, March 24.
Rinsley, D. B. (1977). An object relations view of borderline personalities. In *Borderline Personality Disorders: The Concept, the Syndrome, the Patient,* ed. P. Hartocollis. New York: Int. Univ. Press, pp. 47-70.
Searles, H. F. (1955). Dependency processes in the psychotherapy of schizophrenia. In *Collected Papers on Schizophrenia and Related Subjects.* New York: Int. Univ. Press, 1965, pp. 114-156.
_____ (1959). The effort to drive the other person crazy—an element in the etiology and psychotherapy of schizophrenia. In *Collected Papers on Schizophrenia and Related Subjects.* New York: Int. Univ. Press, 1965, pp. 254-284.
_____ (1963). Transference psychosis in the psychotherapy of schizophrenia. In *Collected Papers on Schizophrenia and Related Subjects.* New York: Int. Univ. Press, 1965, pp. 654-716.
Sifneos, P. E. (1973). The prevalence of "alexithymic" characteristics in psychosomatic patients. *Psychother. and Psychosom.,* 22:255-262.
_____ (1975). Problems of psychotherapy of patients with alexithymic characteristics and physical disease. *Psychother. and Psychosom.,* 26:65-70.
_____ (1977). The phenomenon of "alexithymia." *Psychother. and Psychosom.,* 28:47-57.
Spiegel, J. & Machotka, P. (1974). *Messages of the Body.* New York: Free Press.
Stierlin, H. (1972). Family dynamics in separation patterns of potential schizophrenics. In *Proceedings of the Fourth International Symposium on Psychotherapy of Schizophrenia.* Amsterdam: *Excerpta Medica,* pp. 156-166.
_____ (1973). Group fantasies and family myth—some theoretical and practical aspects. *Fam. Process,* 12:111-125.
Stern, D. (1977). *The First Relationship: Infant and Mother.* Cambridge, MA.: Harvard Univ. Press.
_____ (1983). Implications of infancy research for clinical theory and practice. In *Psychiatry Update, vol. II,* ed. L. Grinspoon. Washington, D.C.: American Psychiatric Press, Inc., pp. 6-21.

Taylor, G. J. (1984). Alexithymia: Concept, measurement, and implication for treatment. *Amer. J. Psychiat.,* 141:725-732.

_____ (1986). *Psychosomatic Medicine and Contemporary Psychoanalysis.* In press.

Thomas, A. & Chess, S. (1980). *The Dynamics of Psychological Development.* New York: Brunner/Mazel.

_____ (1982). Temperament and follow-up to adulthood. In *Temperamental Differences in Infants and Young Children,* ed. R. Porter & G. M. Collins. CIBA Foundation Symposium 89. London: Pitman.

Tustin, F. (1980). Autistic objects. *Int. Rev. Psychoanal.,* 7:27-40.

_____ (1981a). Psychological birth and psychological catastrophe. In *Do I Dare Disturb the Universe? A Memorial to Wilfred R. Bion,* ed. J. S. Grotstein. Beverly Hills: Caesura Press, pp. 181-196.

_____ (1981b). *Autistic States in Children.* London: Routledge & Kegan Paul.

Watson, J. S. (1972). Smiling, cooing, and "the game." *Merrill-Palmer Q. on Behavioral Development,* 18:323-340.

Wender, P. H. & Klein, D. F. (1981). *Mind, Mood, and Medicine.* New York: Farrar, Straus & Giroux.

Wexler, M. (1971). Schizophrenia, conflict, and deficiency. *Psychoanal. Q.,* 40:83-100.

White, R. (1959). Motivation reconsidered: The concept of competence. *Psychol. Rev.,* 66:297-333.

Wilson, R. S. (1978). Synchronies in mental development: An epigenetic perspective. *Science,* 202:939-947.

Winnicott, D. W. (1958). *Collected Papers: Through Paediatrics to Psycho-Analysis.* New York: Basic Books.

_____ (1965). *The Maturational Process and the Facilitating Environment.* New York: Int. Univ. Press.

Wurmser, L. (1981). *The Mask of Shame.* Baltimore/London: The Johns Hopkins Univ. Press.

Wynne, L. C. (1968). The study of intrafamilial alignments and splits in exploratory family therapy. In *Exploring the Base for Family Therapy,* ed. N. W. Ackerman, F. L. Beatman, & S. N. Sherman. New York: Family Serv. Assn., pp. 95-115.

_____ (1969). The family as a strategic focus in cross-cultural psychiatric studies. In *Mental Health Research in Asia and the Pacific,* ed. W. Caudill & T.-Y. Lin. Honolulu: East-West Center Press.

9777 Wilshire Boulevard
Beverly Hills, CA 90212

The Power of the Wish and the Wish for Power: A Discussion of Power and Psychoanalysis

BENNETT SIMON, M.D.

W E ARE PRESENTED HERE with five papers solicited for and submitted for an issue of this journal on the subject of power. The papers, each interesting and valuable in its own right, add up to only a patchwork of contributions to a psychoanalytic overview of power. This discussion, then, will take up primarily the various dimensions of the problem(s) of power and psychoanalysis, and secondarily show the place that these particular papers occupy on that dimensional map.

In order for psychoanalysts to have credibility in discussing power it is crucial to examine why and how psychoanalysts (and psychoanalysis) are interested in power. What is the relationship between psychoanalysis and power? What is the power or the kinds of power we eschew, and for what kinds of power do we yearn but rarely achieve?

Let us consider who writes *about* power? Like many other important things in life, those who have plenty and the assurance of plenty of some commodity tend not to think too much about that commodity, let alone analyze and write it. Lack, not plenty, motivates inquiry. "The strong do what they can, the weak suffer what

Bennett Simon, M.D., is Clinical Associate Professor of Psychiatry, Harvard Medical School (Beth Israel Hospital); Training and Supervising Analyst, Boston Psychoanalytic Society and Institute.

119

they must," proclaims the Athenian speaker cited by Thucydides. We might paraphrase and say, "the strong do what they can, and the weak write about what the strong can do." Thucydides himself, who placed power at the center of his inquiry into history, wrote at a time in his life when he was out of power, and when, in fact, his city-state was in a considerably weakened condition. Machiavelli wrote *The Prince* in part because he was not one. Hitler wrote *Mein Kampf* before he came to power, and, to my knowledge, did not write formally on the subject once he achieved the enormous power he came to wield. It is not entirely the pressures and constraints of office that prevent presidents and prime ministers from writing about their administrations while in office. The relatively unim-powered position of an "ex-" is part of the motivation for such writing. Those in a position to exact revenge upon their enemies do so; those not in such a position dream and/or write about it. Apocalyptic visions about the collapse of powerful empires are the province of those who are the slaves and servants within those empires.

So analysts must first examine their position in relation to the various forms and centers of power that impinge upon them. We once believed we were very powerful, especially in the fifties, sixties, and early seventies, but then we began to experience an erosion of our power base. The surplus of patients seeking analysis changed into a relative shortage, and departments of psychiatry around the country no longer automatically sought psychoanalysts to head them. Today, though the news of our recent death is greatly exaggerated, psychoanalysis could hardly be advertised as a growth industry, a field with enormous promise for influence in the real world.

In sober moments, we eschew any claim that we are powerful, but we do feel that we have some influence. Though we treat only a relatively small number of patients,[1] we believe the patients we treat are able to influence others, that mental health and maturity radiate out in concentric circles from the small pebble we have dropped in

---

[1] John Gedo, a senior training analyst, wrote up a summary of the results of his two decades as a psychoanalyst (1979). By the age of 52, he had treated 36 patients. Assuming another two decades of full-time practice, the number would double to approximately 70 in a lifetime.

the pond in our offices. To my knowledge this claim has never been either substantiated or refuted, and certainly there has never been a compilation of the results of our treatment of important people, highly placed in the political or economic world. We have probably had more experience, perhaps more success, in treating some of the relatives and children of the powerful, some of the casualties of the parental or husbandly climb to, and sojourn at, the pinnacles of power. Whereas in our therapeutic work we have all saved wrecked lives or prevented wreckage, helped deeply troubled people fulfill their considerable potential in love, work, child rearing, and as citizens in the community, this is not a way of obtaining or holding, or brokering power.

Freud had hoped for the eventual triumph of the still small voice of reason over the volcanic destructive forces inherent in man and in civilization and presumably felt that psychoanalysis might contribute a small share to that triumph. This is indeed a most important and stirring hope, perhaps one that helps sustain some of us in our work — that perhaps thereby we might have the power of the lever or of the catalyst. But such power, such spiritual power, is slow in coming and accumulating and is indeed a very fragile creature in a jungle with many powerful and dangerous beasts.

Accordingly, following some of the principles of our theory and of our practice, *lege artis,* we should look for derivative, symbolic, and wish-fulfilling attempts to compensate for that which we do not have, and which, according to our theory, as humans, most of us yearn for. If we as psychoanalysts lack important kinds of power to subjugate and dominate, where and how do we find substitutes? First and foremost, we seek to exercise and practice power within our own field, our organizations, our institutes, and as part of that exercise of power we are continually at war. Some of the warfare is within the family, as it were, and some of it is without — competition with other groups who are not "real analysts," other mental health professionals, and, currently, government officials and insurance companies. The unkindest cut of all is that some of the warfare with other groups is also warfare within the family, for some of us feel injured that we have trained, taught, treated, and even married workers in other mental health fields who now treat us with base ingratitude and law suits.

Freud's "Totem and Taboo," as many now recognize was the first treatise on the nature of psychoanalytic organization, but one must read between the lines to catch the meaning of the work. The Freud-Jung correspondence deals heavily with issues of attaining, maintaining, and balancing power both within the movement and vis-á-vis psychiatry and medicine. The French have written a bit more about these issues within psychoanalysis, as exemplified in the title of Roustang's (1982) study of the psychoanalytic movement, *Dire Mastery*. Russell Jacoby's (1983) controversial book about Otto Fenichel, *The Repression of Psychoanalysis*, has the merit of posing very squarely some issues about politics and psychoanalysis and politics within psychoanalysis. Histories, oral and written, of several psychoanalytic institutes in the United States and the Institute of London, are beginning to document the struggles and passions around power in several major psychoanalytic centers. Certainly the corridors and bedrooms of the hotels where psychoanalytic conventions have been held were and are the scenes of numerous intense, and occasionally thoughtful, discussions about the brokerage and distribution of power. Both friends and enemies of psychoanalysis have suggested that analysts have been "acting out" issues of power among themselves, repeating, as it were, instead of remembering and working through.

But what kind, or kinds, of "analysis" are required to adequately describe and explicate the problems of power within psychoanalysis? Psychoanalysis, as one analytic tool, is an obvious starting point, and much of the thrust of psychoanalytic thinking about the field has been within one or another psychoanalytic framework. But clearly analyses deriving from other vantage points are needed (and have begun to appear in one form or another): group and organizational psychology, Marxist, economic, and social psychological-historical (i.e., the place of the psychoanalytic movement vis-á-vis other twentieth-century movements).

What are the attitudes of psychoanalysts toward those outside the field who attempt to "analyze" the profession? Janet Malcolm's two works (1981, 1983), especially her earlier one, *The Impossible Profession,* were hardly greeted with unanimous enthusiasm by the analytic community. Whatever its biases and problems, which are significant, *The Impossible Profession* is a superb piece of writing about crucial aspects of the practice and organization of analysis. It was not granted the award offered by the American Psychoanalytic Association for journalistic achievement in writing about psychoanalysis, and I wonder what popular work either before or after rivals Malcolm's book in quality and interest. Like other organizations, whether the Democratic Party, the Catholic Church, the Communist Party, the Rotarians, or the Modern Language Association, for psychoanalysis, in-depth critiques from the inside are a bit hard to come by and usually evoke partisan responses; critiques from the outside are viewed ambivalently with both deep interest and deep suspicion. *Quis custodet ipsos custodes?,* who guards the guardians? and the variant in our field, who analyzes the analysts? are extremely painful questions and always difficult to face honestly. Thus who does the analyzing, who confers the authority to analyze and what is the meaning of that act are all vital and typically unaddressed questions. Clearly the contributors to and editors of this journal issue (including, of course, this writer) have motives and needs relating to power that enter into the current enterprise. Just as clearly, probably none of us would have agreed to write were the exploration of our motives a necessary and major part of what we write. Who has empowered us to write and what is the power and influence we hope to achieve by this writing? The exploration and exposition of such motives would obviously fill a large volume and would be most valuable, but it is not likely to be done.

Helen Gediman's "The Plight of the Imposturous Candidate: Learning Amidst the Pressures and Pulls of Power in the Institute," takes cognizance of one aspect of the problem of power within our own analytic organizations. Dr. Gediman, in another context (1984), has written somewhat more extensively about problems of power within psychoanalytic training. Here we find a detailed examination of a problem in psychoanalytic learning and training, the problem of the "imposter." Her hope is, and it is at least partially fulfilled, that a study of this aberrant type will shed light on the ordinary processes and pressures within psychoanalytic institutes. Her allusions to the power structure and the role of institutional issues in the intrapsychic conflicts of candidates is important and at times painful. What is the optimal amount and kind of authority that fosters analytic learning and development, and what kinds of authority, or abdication of authority interfere with and pervert such learning? It is a contribution, indeed, toward the larger issue I raise of the relationship of psychoanalysts and psychoanalysis to power and to the quest for domination. Her discussion ought at some point to be expanded in relation to the problem of the patient who is being treated by a disturbed candidate. The patient is in many ways the most powerless person within analytic institutes. Is not the patient entitled to sue for damages, return of fees, restitution of some sort for the institute assigning to her a defective therapist and for allowing her to continue in treatment? Patients are already beginning to take such questions in their own hands.

To return to the task of looking for substitute gratifications: within ourselves, certainly a major one is that of psychoanalysis applied to studying the world of political and economic power. Many years ago Gedo (1970) wrote a paper on the enterprise of psychoanalysis applied to literature, "The Psychoanalyst and the Literary Hero: An Interpretation." In brief, he argued that psychoanalysts tend to be *artistes manques,* writers and creators in their daydreams but not in actuality, and that some of us—present company included—turn to writing about writing as a consolation, and often may seek vicarious power and acclaim by identification with the great writers (and with the heroes and heroines within the writing). For myself, were I able to compose the equivalent of one speech in Shakespeare or ten lines of Homer, I would gladly forgo all my written and unwritten studies of these geniuses. So, then, are we thrown back on *envy* as one major motive force in leading psychoanalysts (as well as a few historians, political scientists, and economists) to write about psychodynamic aspects of power, with a capital "P"? One could list other motives, but we must also keep in mind another rule of our analytic art, that the final product must be judged by criteria other than the motives that went into it. Aristotle (*Ethics*) and Freud (cf. the end of "The Interpretation of Dreams," p. 621) agreed that actions and not wishes are the touchstone of a man's worth and moral caliber.

There is a long history within psychoanalysis of the study of politics and political figures, and the results are at best mixed, whether judged by the most ardent supporters, or most strident opponents of the enterprise. Peter Gay (1985) has provided us with a summary and appraisal of this line of inquiry, and Stannard (1980) offers a widely read and generally enthusiastically received negative appraisal. "Psychohistory" begins, I believe, with Freud's own "political dreams" (1900) — Count Thun, dreams about Rome and Hannibal, the dream of Bismarck, etc. (see Schorske, 1973).

Two of the articles in this study, the study of Catherine dé Medici by Abby Adams-Silvan and Mark Silvan, and Peter Loewenberg's comments on the careers of Nixon and Hitler, are judicious attempts to bring psychoanalytic insights into play in studying the careers of major political figures. These articles raise important questions about method and results in applying psychoanalytic approaches to the lives of political figures. They raise the question of how one integrates psychoanalytically based or psychoanalytically derived explanations (i.e., here I mean primarily "instinct and defense" formulations) with explanations deriving from other frameworks, whether the framework is economic, or "common sense" psychology, or some sort of theory of historical forces and of historical contingencies. Peter Loewenberg argues explicitly for the need to pose ego-psychological questions about the behavior of leaders, as well as instinct and defense formulations. Adams-Silvan and Silvan implicitly acknowledge this need, while usefully exploring how far an explanation in the language of psychosexual development can take us. Closer examination of what Loewenberg means by "ego functioning" leads to the realization that both psychoanalytic and nonpsychoanalytic explanations must be invoked in a mixture and ratio impossible to determine a priori and inevitably subject to controversy *a posteriori*. The more elaborate and psychoanalytically sophisticated the explanation of Hitler's behavior

becomes, the more complex the question about what is the unique
power of psychoanalytic explanation in history. I do not fault
Loewenberg or Adams-Silvan and Silvan for not definitively an-
swering such questions, for the answers must come in large part
with conducting historical studies *pari passu* with continually raising the important methodological issues. But my point is that even
in the best of the products of "psychohistory" the demonstration of
the power native to psychoanalytic explanation and exploration vis-
á-vis other kinds of explanation is by no means trivial or obvious.

Ethel Person's "Male Sexuality and Power" and James Grotstein's "The Psychology of Powerlessness" bring us to the realm of
psychoanalysis as a clinical discipline and as a theoretical enterprise
oriented toward understanding the clinical situation. Though Person's questionnaire — derived material — and her clinical material
are interesting, I shall not focus on their content, but rather on
some of her assumptions and methods as they relate to the study of
power. For example, she illustrates a common and important aspect of psychoanalytic thinking about abnormal mental functioning, namely, that it might show us something about the "normal" and the "ordinary." Those men for whom sexual domination
is a primary concern generally reveal particular conflicts in their
sexual development. However, the nature of their unconscious conflicts as revealed in analyses are useful in ascertaining the "fault"
line in more typical (or "normal") male development. Arguing from
what she defines as a not entirely typical group of men, she proposes "to place power and domination concerns into perspective by
proposing that control over the penis and the sexual object are central concerns in male sexuality, more fundamental than the problem of aggression and intimately intertwined with the genesis of castration anxiety." ("Every man in Budapest has two penises, his own
and one that is really terrific" goes a psychoanalytic-Hungarian
aphorism.) Thus we see one kind of power that psychoanalytically
clinically based hunches provide, the power to generalize from a
small and distinctively "pathological" group to a larger, more heterogeneous, and more "normal" group. The assumption is so fundamental to psychoanalytic thinking about the normal and the ordinary, that, on the whole, it is the critics of psychoanalysis who tend

to call that assumption into question, albeit often for defensive reasons of their own. I would see this as a methodological assumption
that is a powerful and useful starting point, a hypothesis-generating
method, but not a final resting place in explanation. Another form
of psychoanalytic exploratory and explanatory power is seen in one
of Person's overarching purposes of the paper, namely, to call into
question certain popular and clinical stereotypes about male sexuality, power needs and aggression. "Sadism ought not to be considered the norm among men any more than masochism is viewed as
the norm among women," she concludes. Again, while I concur
with her conclusion (or rather, hope and assume it is true) her clinical findings are *starting points* for such a generalization, not the
end point. Further methods of more general testing of such state-
ments are needed before we can, more or less, rest content with their
validity. These more general points apart, I do find her formulation
about the role of anxiety about the control of the penis in some men
as clinically valid, original, and useful in trying to formulate a more
general and global schema about male sexuality and male power
needs.

Person's paper also points up an important and "native" psychoanalytic aspect of the study of power, namely, that "power" is not a
unitary concept, that each person (specifically each patient) has a
particular version and vision of what power is, wherein it lies, who
or what possesses it, and what are the forms of power that count in
life. A young woman with phobias dreamed of passing and failing
courses, getting a "P" instead of a "D." She emphasized that in the
dream these were upper-case and not lower-case letters. "P" has a
tail, and not just a hole, as does "D," and "P" stands for power, potency and penis. She later realized that in lower-case letters and in
handwriting, neither letter has a clear "advantage" over the other,
but that they may be mirror-images or complementary forms. A
psychoanalytic contribution to the study of power, then, is to emphasize that the difficulty of defining power has much to do with
the vicissitudes of individual *fantasies* about power.

Grotstein's title, "The Psychology of Powerlessness: Disorders of
Self-Regulation and Interactional Regulation as a Newer Paradigm
for Psychopathology," suggests at once the ambiguous position his

paper occupies in a volume devoted to psychoanalysis and power. This formidable and rich contribution must be reworked so as to show its significant connection with issues of power (a reworking that I believe would be quite rewarding). What is essentially an essay on how to conceptualize primitive mental states and primitive personalities tends to equate "powerlessness" with "weakness of the ego" of "defect" or "deficiency." Grotstein's formulations, to my mind, are more successful in highlighting important questions about the development of a sense of effectence, competence, and various kinds of personal sense of power than they are in providing answers to these questions. His discussions of alexithymia and of contentless affect-states, or somato-affective states ("actual neurosis") are very suggestive, but they point to major issues and major lacunae in our understanding of the relationship between the verbal, the affective, and the symbolic. His discussion of *symbolizing* as a way for the psyche to gain power, via making a myth, or a story, is intriguing and warrants amplification. Clearly, the bulk of his discussion treats of the presymbolic and structural components of the sense of personal effectence and power.

There is another hint in this paper worth elaboration and worth arguing, namely, that certain terms in psychoanalytic theory may be covert terms about power, even perhaps political power. Various Marxist critics of psychoanalysis are fond of arguing that terms such as *drive* and *energy* are expressions of political and class-based ideologies, that psychoanalytic theoretic treatises are in fact about distribution and control within the body politic and not only the body–psyche combination. Dr. Grotstein could do us a service by exploring these overtones of both older and newer theoretical vocabulary.

But overall, the center of gravity of his paper is not around the issue of power in any ordinary sense of the term. This paper, meritorious as it is in important respects as a contribution to the study of power, demonstrates that what psychoanalysts seem to mean by "power" is so variable, so heterogeneous, and refers to so many different realms of individual and cultural experience as to almost make a mockery of the claim that there is, or are, psychoanalytic perspectives on power.

Let me conclude this slightly querulous catalogue of what has not been included and discussed in this collection of essays with reflections on another aspect of the craft of psychoanalysis. What is the kind of power that the analyst seeks, or the kinds of power that analysts seek, in being analysts and in particular in the practice of psychoanalysis—these are questions that have been asked many times over the decades, often in the course of the analysis of the person who is becoming an analyst. A humorous skit in a medical school class show depicted the admissions office of the medical school, with an anxious applicant pacing up and down, saying: "What am I going to tell them when they ask me why I want to be a doctor—I just can't tell them the real reasons—money, power, and the wish to see naked woman free—I've got to come up with some better reasons!" When I refer to "what kinds of power" I am asking an ego-psychological question, or asking for a catalogue of motives in terms of degree of instinctual push and in terms of degree of "sublimation" "neutralization," and also mastery of conflict. I am raising these questions also from a point of neutrality, as it were, among ego, id, and superego, not biased in advance for or against pushes and motives emanating from any of the psychic agencies. A male analyst in the course of analyzing women may be simultaneously mastering his fears of female sexuality, providing considerable help to his patient, and perhaps even becoming aware of feelings and issues in himself and in his patient that may enhance our theory and practical understanding of female sexuality. Similarly, with a female analyst and male patients, as in Dr. Person's paper, propelled by a variety of motives, the analyst may arrive at important new twists, or new insights into the nature of male sexuality. I would welcome a contribution on the grades and varieties of power motives of analysts in becoming analysts, a paper that would be a start in organizing what anecdotally and personally we all know, but what has never been adequately collected and described.

The setting of this discussion of a group of articles on "Power" for a journal of psychoanalytic inquiry includes my having just used this same word processor to write several letters relating to the case of Dr. Anatoly Koryagin. Dr. Koryagin is a Russian psychiatrist imprisoned in Central Russia for having refused to certify a number of political dissidents as mentally ill and in need of hospitalization. My writing of letters is an attempt by someone in a politically powerless position to influence some very powerful people to act in favor of a person who is in a desperately powerless situation. Powerless politically and personally. One small consolation for Dr. Koryagin (and perhaps for myself and the readers of this discussion) is that those in power in the Soviet Union must somehow consider that Dr. Koryagin possesses or can mobilize a significant amount of power, and that power makes him dangerous enough to incarcerate and punish severely while in prison.

Finally, I do regret the absence of one more area, close to the concerns I raised in the opening paragraphs of this essay. I refer to the question (for which I do not have the answer) of what is the power, or what are the powers, of psychoanalysts to contribute to that process by which "the still small voice" of reason may prevail over the destructive and annihilative propensities of the species homo sapiens. My bias is that an analysis of the relatively powerless state of psychoanalysis vis-á-vis the world is not a statement of grounds for resignation, but rather a starting point in working through our defenses and illusions about our own power and powerlessness to effect changes in the world. Such a dialectic and such a process of working through is taking place in all of us to some degree, but it is urgent for us as analysts to advance our own understanding of ourselves as political creatures, influenced by but also capable of influencing the dreadful course of events that can lead to total obliteration of the whole race, including both the analyzed, the imperfectly analyzed, and the never analyzed.

REFERENCES

Freud, S. (1900). The interpretation of dreams. *S.E.*, 4 & 5.
Gay, P. (1985). *Freud for Historians.* New York: Oxford Univ. Press.
Gedo, J. (1970). The psychoanalyst and the literary hero: An interpretation. In *Comprehensive Psychiat.*, 1:174–181.
————— (1979). A psychoanalyst reports at mid-career. *Amer. J. Psychiat.*, 136(5): 646–649.
Jacoby, R. (1983). *The Repression of Psychoanalysis: Otto Fenichel and the Political Freudians.* New York: Basic Books.

Malcolm, J. (1981). *Psychoanalysis: The Impossible Profession.* New York: Knopf.
_____ (1983). *In the Freud Archives.* New York: Knopf.
Roustang, F. (1982). *Dire Mastery. Discipleship from Freud to Lacan,* trans. N. Lukacher. Baltimore/London: Johns Hopkins Univ. Press.
Schorske, C. F. (1973). Politics and parricide in Freud's "The Interpretation of Dreams." *Annual Psychoanal.,* 2:40–60.
Stannard, D. E. (1980). *Shrinking History: On Freud and the Failure of Psychohistory.* New York: Oxford Univ. Press.

170 Chestnut Street
West Newton, MA. 02165

Epilogue

OUR PIONEERING EFFORT to bring the concept of power into the mainstream of psychoanalytic inquiry has led to contributions diverse in subject and formulation. Nonetheless, when the papers are viewed as a whole, a predominant theme emerges: current psychoanalytic reliance on theories of aggression and sadism, on anxiety and defense, are inadequate to deal with the causality and phenomenology of power. A psychoanalytic study of power requires a comprehensive consideration of ego functions (Loewenberg), deficits in self and ego regulation (Grotstein and Person), interaction (Gediman), and the consolidation of sexual identity (Adams-Silvan and Silvan). In an earlier issue Meissner (1985) stated that, despite criticisms and proposed alternatives, traditional metapsychology offers the greatest promise for the assimilation of complete intrapsychic and interactional viewpoints. Detailed analytic study of concepts like power that bridge these points of view provide a challenging test for Meissner's hypothesis.

REFERENCE

Meissner, W. W. (1985). Psychoanalysis: The dilemma of science and humanism. *Psychoanal. Inquiry*, 5:471–498.

Melvin Bornstein, M.D.
Issue Editor

TOPICS OF FUTURE ISSUES

Aggression and Its Alternatives in the Field of International Relations

Commentaries on Kohut's *How Does Analysis Cure?*

A Reappraisal of Heinz Hartmann's Contributions

The Structural Model in Clinical Psychoanalysis

The Application of Infant Research

The Psychoanalysis of Young Adults

Transference and Transference Neurosis

Sibling Relationships

Commentaries on Abend, Willick, and Horder's *Borderline Patients: Psychoanalytic Perspectives*

The Developmental Perspective

Mind, Body, Brain

Methodology of Research

Pregnancy

Change in Psychoanalysis

Anxiety Hysteria